The Hidden Power of Productivity

Improving Productivity by 30%
without layoffs!

A business novel

by

Fintan William Bohan

GUARANTEE

If, after applying the principles described in this book, your business does not generate a return of at least 1,000 times your investment in purchasing the book, I will return your money.

The Author

authorHOUSE™

1663 LIBERTY DRIVE, SUITE 200
BLOOMINGTON, INDIANA 47403
(800) 839-8640
WWW.AUTHORHOUSE.COM

First published by AuthorHouse 11/19/04

ISBN: 1-4184-8468-7 (sc)

Printed in the United States of America
Bloomington, Indiana

This book is printed on acid-free paper.

Table of Contents

ACKNOWLEDGEMENTS

I would like to thank the following people who have been instrumental in guiding me and providing me with the knowledge and experiences which have culminated in this book.

My first expression of gratitude goes to my parents, Peggy and Gerry, who have unwaveringly supported and loved me, even though I have chosen often to work and live many thousands of miles from my origins. And to my dear wife, Martha, who has had to endure many weeks raising our 3 children alone as I traveled between the U.K., Southern Africa and Latin America.

People who have supported and guided me through my professional career and made a mark that I can still feel somewhere in my heart, include former bosses or colleagues, people of positive influence outside of my consultancy activities, and my clients.

In the first group, I would like to thank Tony Hardwick, Gene Awde, Ralph Brunswick, Richard Steele, and Mario Hermosilla, former bosses or colleagues who taught me to believe in myself and provided me with many opportunities for growth and learning;

In the second group I would like to mention Philip Ray for persuading me to train as a '7 Habits' facilitator and Marta Sanchez for reams of wonderful advice on delivery of training programmes; Marcial Cortés of Fundación Chile for his patience and persistence which resulted in my family relocating to work in that beautiful country, Chile; Enrique Cibié for being a beacon and role model of unfailing optimism in the face of adversity; and Sid Joynson for opening my eyes to a better and much more humane way of doing productivity improvement consultancy.

The third group is the largest. I have learnt more from my clients than I surely was able to teach them, and I feel a profound gratitude and humility for having the fortune of being able to work with these gifted people. From the U.K., the names Malcolm Reading and Brian Bush come fondly to memory; from South Africa, Willem Olivier and Mike Janssen of Sappi, André de Nyschen and Gordon Scott from Murray and Roberts; and from Mexico, Newton de Oliviera (even though he's Brazilian) of Aga. The list from Chile is naturally longer as I have spent the last 8 years of my life here: Sergio Muñoz, my first client here, at the time manager of the Celulosa Arauco plant; Richard Cheney, former Managing Director of Blue Circle's operations in Chile; Jorge Serón of the Arauco Forestry Company; Gerardo Maria and Juan Luis Kostner, of the Banco Sudamericano; and Juan Rassmuss (for the project in his company Cimet in Argentina).

Once we started Trinity, it was at first difficult to persuade Companies that we could help improve productivity without laying people off, and so I owe a special thanks to those people who were willing to take this leap of faith with me, and allow me to practice in their companies. This list includes: Alfredo Schiappacasse, the Managing Director of Terramater Wine Company, who I must salute as the first to take the leap; Martin Flannery and José Miguel Camus of Clée Fruit exporters; Pierre Traverso of Bosques Arauco; Alex Ruf of Cholguán Woodmills, Gonzalo Claverie and Raúl Noguera of Viña Errazuriz Wine Company; Arturo Roa of the insurance giant, Consorcio Nacional de Seguros; Roberto Ordoñez of Rhein Office Products; Javier Mozo and Marcelo Meneghello of Marinetti Packaging; and Carlos Jerez of Editorial Trineo.

INTRODUCTION

I would like to be able to say that I invented the techniques in this book, but that would be untrue. My role has just been a synergizer, blending different technologies from different sources, and arriving at a result that is more than the sum of each separately. As best as I can tell, the evolution of these methods is as follows.

In the late 1940's, a young consultant by the name of Alexander Proudfoot was on an assignment at a mail-order company in Chicago, in the months before the Christmas rush period. As Christmas drew ever closer, he observed panic and stress levels rising, as orders kept coming in, and the backlog of orders to be dispatched kept on rising. When the backlog hit 5 weeks, precisely 5 weeks before Christmas, chaos broke out. It would be impossible to ship all the orders taken, because the postal service was traditionally swamped during those weeks and normally only guaranteed delivery when posted at least 2 weeks before Christmas. Customers were constantly ringing up to get confirmation that their orders would arrive before Christmas, further diverting the staff's time from preparing the shipments. Hundreds of cancellations started to come in, and a pile of legal demands for refunds on mislaid orders kept on growing.

Drastic situations sometimes call for drastic solutions. The normal way of working was to assign a bunch of orders to each picker to pick simultaneously. Someone had an idea. Gather all the orders into one place in the warehouse and give the smallest number of orders possible to each picker. Somebody else suggested that the smallest number of orders to be handled by one picker is the number of orders that could be picked in 20 minutes. Therefore, if there was a problem, any order could then be traced in less than 20 minutes.

Three weeks before Christmas there were no orders left to pick. The Vice President sent the workers home early.

The next day by noon, the same thing happened. The day following, the warehouse had run out of work by 11.30 am. The Vice President panicked, thinking that people had stopped sending orders, and gave instructions to fire half the staff.

The next day they ran out of work again by 2.00 pm. The Vice President, in a state of terror, gave instructions to fire half the remainder.

Up until Christmas all other orders received in the day were shipped that same day by one quarter of the original staff.

The Vice President could not bear to look at his figures, believing that his staff had run out of work because customers had stopped sending their orders in. He convinced himself that it was only a question of time before someone from Head Office came to tell him that he was fired.

When the Chairman turned up on the day before Christmas Eve, the Vice President started to offer his apologies. He was cut short by the Chairman, who asked him if he knew that he had dispatched more products in that month than in any month in the whole history of the Company.

The 20-minute control period became standard in the mail order business.

The consultant, Alexander Proudfoot, who had observed this process, became fascinated with the idea. He set up his own Company and tried the idea out in a foundry. After trial and error, he decided that 20 minutes was too short for that business, and 1 hour would be sufficient. Within two months, the foundry was producing double with half the workforce, a 300% productivity increase!

Proudfoot called the technique Short Interval Scheduling (SIS). Over the years the principles were adapted and improved to handle indirect areas and service industries, such as banks, insurance companies, hospitals, research scientists, computer programmers, designers, stockbrokers, actuaries, etcetera, always showing impressive results.

To reduce the technique to its bare essence, ask yourself (or better still, get your boss to ask you) the following:

What have you done in the last hour, 2 hours, half day, and day?

What did you plan to do?

What prevented you from achieving your plan?

What can I do to help you to eliminate that problem?

What do you plan to do in the next hour, 2 hours, half day, and day?

Can I get anything prepared for you?

Teamwork is important here. It is often better to get someone else to ask these questions. This person should be someone whose opinion you value and won't let you cheat in your answers, just as a high level sports coach will not go soft on his trainees.

Alexander Proudfoot made himself a multi-millionaire and did the same for his partners in his Company based in Palm Beach, Florida, USA. From its origins in the States, the Proudfoot Company spread first to Canada and then across the globe.

I joined the Proudfoot Company in Europe in 1984, directly after my Master's Degree in Engineering, and was assigned to a project which could not be more different than my studies: a chain of 200 newsagents across England, where the objective was to increase productivity and sales. Within a very short period, I saw the impact of SIS applied to this industry. The first branch where I had to install the system was in the Arndale Shopping Center in Manchester, with a relatively young and inexperienced Branch Manager (although he had more experience than me in his industry!). This branch was ranked in the bottom quarter of the monthly branch rankings, i.e. was normally in the bottom 50 of the 200 branches. The Branch Manager and I were both young and enthusiastic, and worked hard during a short installation period of 3 days. The result was that the Arndale branch shot up the league table to occupy the 8th position within that same month! Some weeks later, I experienced another live example of the power of the system. It was mid-November and we were installing at a branch in Liverpool. I mention the month because in winter in England it gets dark early, and this background detail is relevant to what happened. The system we were installing gave us information at regular 2-hour intervals (in this case, not the one hour interval referred to earlier) on sales takings, sales per employee, average amount sold per customer, man-hours worked, customers per man-hour, etcetera. At 10 am, 12 pm and 2 pm, the system said that the £sales, £sales per customer, and customers per man-hour figures were all spot on plan. It should be noted that the plan incorporated a significant improvement over the previous year's figures, and we were achieving it! But something happened to put us off track. At the 4pm check, the Branch Manager and I noticed from the system that £sales takings the last 2 hours had dropped dramatically! There was no apparent reason. The shelves were all well stocked with product. All of the sales staff were present to attend customers, so it was not as if customers were not spending because nobody was attending them. No lost sales were reported. The average £sales per customer were above plan, which meant that as the customers were coming in, the staff were applying the sales techniques we had taught them. But the strange thing was that the system informed us that the number of customers was abruptly down on plan from 2 pm onwards. Neither the staff nor we could fathom why. The Branch Manager went to the shops on either side to ask them if they had noticed a similar problem, but they reported that they found things very much as usual. To clear our heads, we went for a walk outside the branch. As we got to the other side of the road, looking back at the shop, we noticed something curious. The shops on either side of ours were all brightly lit, while ours was in semi-darkness. What had happened was that as it gets dark slowly, and people get accustomed to it, no one had thought of switching the lights on. There was still enough light inside the branch to work comfortably. But from across the street, against the bright lights of our neighbors, it looked like our branch was closed! Perhaps people were just walking on by, because they thought we weren't open? We went back across, entered the shop, turned on the lights, and then witnessed the turnaround. By the 6pm check, the system reported that we were back on plan on all indicators, that the number of customers had returned to its expected level, and had indeed recovered the loss by 6pm!

This was my first project experience with Proudfoot. Followed a project in a steel mill in France, then a project in Singapore with Philips Electronics, where I saw a 30 % improvement in productivity generated in the first day of the installation of the new production control system based on SIS!

It was my experience that the Proudfoot Company did not publish its methodology, for the obvious reason that the secrets of the methodology were too profitable. However, it did produce a great number of spin-off companies, all purporting to do the same thing but better. After 2 years with Proudfoot, I left to join one of the spin-offs, where I spent a further 11 years. During this time I also had brief sojourns with two other 'look-a-likes', and came into contact with many others. I learnt that one common feature of the majority of these companies, which went under the banner of 'implementation management consultants', was that the productivity improvement programmes very often resulted in layoffs of as much as 20% or 30% of the workforce. This was at a time before the terms 're-engineering' and 'downsizing' had become part of everyday business speech. But by the end of the 80's and throughout the 90's, softer approaches to productivity improvement were being presented, such as empowerment, quality circles, competencies, the 7 Habits, and many others. This meant that it became increasingly more difficult to sell the 'hard' approach, often unpopular with managements as it forces them to confront Unions and manage large-scale redundancies. It also meant that the SIS approach was unpopular with workers and Unions, and because it is associated with the painful experience of laying off people, it has fallen out of use in many companies once the savings had been achieved and the consultants had left.

It appears that now the softer technologies are taking the terrain once held firmly by the implementation-style companies. More and more business leaders are looking for ways of improving their results in the long term, without inflicting the deep psychological wounds and the consequent loss of trust and confidence between management and workers that can result from a short term strategy of employee layoffs.

During 1997, after having read Steven Covey's book, 'The 7 Habits of Highly Effective People', I went on a 3-day '7 Habits Workshop'. One of the exercises in this programme is writing down a personal mission in life. I thought that I had my personal mission pretty much clear in my head, but writing it down crystallized it in a more powerful way. I knew in my heart at that moment that I would be leaving my employer company to practice what I considered to be a more humane form of productivity consultancy. I came to the personal realization that there were probably several thousands of people spread out over 8 countries where I had worked who had lost their jobs through my direct or indirect involvement. In a very personal moment, I resolved that my income would no longer depend upon other people losing their jobs. I further resolved that, whereas in the past I had caused many thousands of people to lose their jobs, the future focus of my work would be to help many thousands of people grow within organizations, as a route to helping those organizations become more productive and more profitable.

In 1998, I left the company where I had worked 11 years, determined to develop an approach to productivity improvement consultancy with which I felt comfortable. I had previously met Sid Joynson, who in his book and BBC TV series called 'Sid's Heroes: 30% productivity improvement in 2 days' shows a more humane approach to productivity improvement. What Sid basically does is take a group of 20 or so workers, and in the space of a 2 or 3 day Workshop, he trains them in techniques ordinarily used by external consultants, with the result that the workers are able to present to senior management at the end of the Workshop dramatic productivity improvements in their own areas. But in order for this to have credibility with the workforce, Sid demands that the General Manager commits to not firing anybody as a result of any measures proposed by the Workshop. After long international telephone conversations, Sid invited me to England to see how he did things there, and after a short while suggested that I had seen enough, that I should return to Chile and design a program for that culture. That is consequently what I did with the help of my partners and some very loyal and helpful clients. We developed an equivalent of the "Sid's Heroes'" workshops for a Latin culture (we called them Champions' Workshops as the word 'heroes' often has an undesirable military connotation in Latin America) and implemented them with great success and personal satisfaction at several companies. Towards the end of 1988, I had the opportunity to put into effect an adaptation of the Sid approach at a small door manufacturing Company of some 28 people. Within six weeks we had increased production from 22 doors a day to 45! Encouraged by this, I continued to develop the workshops. One of our clients, Roberto Ordoñez of Rhein, an office products company, suggested to us that we combine the strength of Sid's people-based approach with the many 'hard' tools used in the traditional productivity improvement consultancy. This gave rise to the Trinity programme *'Unleashing People Power'*, which is the main thrust of this book. The programme was tried and tested at Rhein, where the results were a more than 50% productivity improvement and a dramatic improvement in customer service without any resultant layoffs!

This book focuses on those parts of the 'hard' technology that can be usefully incorporated into a productivity improvement programme that has its objective growing people as a route to growing profits, rather than cutting them. For that reason, no discussion is given to the techniques known as 'manloading' here. Manloading refers to the process where the work content is analyzed by the consultants, in order to redesign an area to function with less people producing the same level of volume. In our experience, it is much more powerful to teach a group of workers how to 'man load' their own area. During the Rhein project, after we had reorganized a particular production area to work with less people, producing more, giving a productivity improvement of 42%, I had the opportunity to train some of the workers from that same area in some simple manloading techniques during a Champions' Workshop. They consequently redesigned their area to deliver another 30% productivity improvement, over and above what we had already done! But to achieve this, there was a key difference. I had asked Roberto, the General Manager, to give a guarantee that there would be no layoffs as a result of the training and any initiative it produced! If a manager genuinely respects his people, as does Roberto, then this is not a problem. Achieving the results without this, however, would be like plucking a hen's teeth! As an old saying in England goes: "You don't ask the turkeys to vote for Christmas!"

So why am I publishing these techniques now when no one has, to my knowledge, published them before? Well, firstly, through better personal organization, I made the time for myself to do so. Many others perhaps have had the desire, but have not been as fortunate in their time availability. Secondly, I believe that each of us has a responsibility to help make the world we live in a better place. I know, and can guarantee that if every company were to apply these principles we would all be receiving products and services much cheaper and quicker and at higher quality than before, thereby improving the standard of living and increasing the material abundance available for everyone. And finally, in most countries, about 80% of the companies are classified as SMEs (Small-to-Medium Enterprises), and are unable to afford this type of consultancy due to the high fees involved. But it is true that the economic growth of any country depends on these companies far more than the much fewer large corporations. So, in order to help stimulate growth, I am making these techniques readily available to those companies which most benefit from them, at a fraction of the cost of hiring an outside consultant. I can foresee University undergraduates applying these techniques in SMEs during their industrial training periods. It is my hope that the widespread application of these techniques in S.M.E.s can add a few percentage points permanently to the growth rates of many countries.

Chapter 1: The journey starts

"Well, that settles that. We've agreed your starting package, your goals for the first year, how you will be measured and how often, and your start date. All that remains now is for you to get started, Andy. Welcome to SportsBall Inc." With these words, Bill Braces extended his hand towards me, and I grasped it in a firm handshake, grinning like a puppy. The time I had spent researching Bill and his Company had just paid off.

"Thank you sir, I think we will have a long and successful career together."

Bill Braces is General Manager, SportsBall Inc. He is also the founder, and majority owner. I found Bill's and the company's history fascinating as I researched it. It all started with Bill designing and assembling balls in his own garage some 30 years ago during his spare time, and selling them himself and through a group of sports fanatic salesmen. These were the two driving features of the company: its high quality crafted products and the dynamism of its sales force. The company had grown over the years, different products being added. All of the management systems had been designed by Bill or one of his associates, as the need arose or a specific problem developed over the years. Within 5 years, SportsBall had set up its own manufacturing facility, which grew steadily in capacity over the following 25 years. But invariably, as new capacity was added, it was almost always soon afterwards running at 100%.

Whenever additional capacity was required, the production overflow was farmed out to a wide net of subcontract firms. And this was quite frequent, as the specialized sports-fanatic sales force, which had become famous all over the continent, often sent orders into the plant which exceeded its installed capacity. SportsBall currently sells a range of 150 products, grouped for convenience into four product families: footballs, volleyballs, rugby balls and tennis balls. Now approaching his seventies, Bill Braces was looking to bring some new blood into the organization. For that reason, SportsBall Inc has just hired a new aggressive Production Manager, none other than yours truly, Andy Case. Actually, this being my first step on the managerial ladder, you can bet that I'm going to give it everything. Since leaving University, I had worked for SportsBall's main competitor in the industry, UniBallCo. Whereas SportsBall was number one in the market, with 55% market share, it is a relatively small company with 350 employees, while UniBallCo, even though being smaller, with only 30% market share, was part of a large international manufacturing group, with vast resources. After starting on a general management trainee programme, where I went from department to department for almost a year, then I settled down into production supervision, and quickly worked my way up to Assistant Production Manager. I was set on a corporate career, but Bill offered me the chance to be a "bigger fish in a small pond", with share options dependent on performance. I reasoned that I was too many years away from being able to achieve something similar within UniBallCo, and so I was ready to take him up on his offer.

During the interviews, Bill had gone to great pains to stress to me that one of our prime goals would be to improve the productivity of the plant by a minimum of 30% during the next two years. The company used to boast that it had the best productivity, but Bill now feels that we are slipping in customer service, losing business to our competitors, and according to industry-published statistics, we have lost ground on productivity too. Bill feels that the two are somehow related, in other words it is not just a coincidence that customer service has slipped while productivity has dropped. My job is to fix the problem, and to reverse the trend. So, when I arrived at the Company to take up my new position some weeks later,

I set about my new responsibilities with gusto. Bill introduced me to my production supervisors: Jimmy from Preparation, Jack from Cutting, Barry from Stitching & Shaping, Jon from Assembly, and Willy from Packing. During our 'get to know each other' meeting, Bill explained that he hired me to help bring about a 30% productivity improvement, and that he counted on each one of them to give me the fullest support. After presenting me, Bill left me to it and I got down to business straight away.

Now, after 9 months, I feel proud of our achievements: we have organized product flows, laying out the factory into discrete areas; we have proper job descriptions and a salary structure; we have a stable and motivated team of supervisors; staff turnover is down 35%; the cost of the main raw material, leather, has been successfully negotiated down by 5%; we have a productivity and quality bonus scheme in place and the factory now is a tidy and professional-looking place. While I feel there is still a lot to do, the foundations are in place, and the supervisors and I are happy to be able to report a 5% productivity increase, measured in balls produced per manhour.

They say that when your bubble is too inflated, along comes something to pop it. And this is exactly what now happens to me. The pin prick is a call to a meeting with Bill: "I want to review our productivity with you. According to my figures, we have dropped 5 percentage points since you got here. Can you come to my office, now?".

On the way up to Bill's office, my head is spinning. Have we calculated wrong? No, it can't be that, we've checked those calculations four times, at least! And the supervisors are always eagle-eyed on the productivity calculations since they were put on a productivity bonus! And as soon as I conclude this, I find myself outside Bill's office.

Entering Bill's office, I decide to take the bull by the horns: "Bill, what is this nonsense about productivity dropping by 5%? Don't you mean to say it's up by 5%? Look, here are our latest figures!"

Bill looks at me searchingly as I hand over the sheets which I had hurriedly printed off. They show the following:

CUMULATIVE PRODUCTION STATISTICS: JAN -SEPT.

	Last Year	This Year	% difference
Balls produced	1,005,035	1,058,302	+5.3%
Manhours	2,000,500	2,000,100	
Ratio: balls/hour	0.50	0.529	+5.7%

Bill studies the figures in silence for what seems an enormously long time. He scribbles some calculations on a pad, referring to my figures. Finally, he looks up at me and says: "Andy, I'm now going to teach you how I look at productivity from a business perspective, not just a narrow production focus. Are you ready?"

I nod affirmative.

This time Bill hands me his pad. His figures show:

YEAR-TO DATE SALES STATISTICS: JAN -SEPT.

	Last Year	This Year	% difference
Sales	$10,006,935	$9,458,302	-5.5%
Manhours	2,000,500	2,000,100	
Sales/manhour	$ 5.0	$ 4.73	-5.4%

"Maybe one day you hope to progress from being the Production Manager to the General Manager of a Company. Am I right?"

I acknowledge that Bill is right in this supposition.

"In that case, it would pay you to consider the Company-wide situation, not just your individual area. I've just taken some of your figures here, and related them to our sales value. What do they show?"

"They seem to show that we are selling 5% less for every manhour worked here. But how can this be?"

"Because competition is tougher, both from local and imported products, margins are tighter, and consequently prices have reduced." Bill explains.

I look at Bill's pad again, and then look again at the sheets I brought to the meeting. "Bill, will you allow me a few minutes to look at another calculation on your pad?"

"Sure, go ahead, I'll make a call and order some coffee meanwhile".

It strikes me that we need to look more deeply at how Bill's figures and mine overlap. I produce the following table, using some of his and some of my information.

COMBINED PRODUCTION AND SALES STATISTICS: JAN -SEPT.

	Last Year	This Year	% difference
Sales	$10,006,935	$9,458,302	-5.5%
Balls produced	1,005,035	1,058,302	+5.3%
Sales value/ball	$9.957	$8.937	-10.24%

"Bill, this is horrendous. According to this, we are selling our balls for 10% less than we were last year!"

"That is exactly what I've been trying to tell you, Andy. While you are apparently sitting pretty in Production, satisfied with a 5 % productivity increase, our business is going to the cleaners".

I suddenly feel humbled. "How much of this is a result of changing the mix of the products we sell?"

"Well, it's a fact that we are selling more tennis balls now, which are our lowest priced items, and selling less footballs, which are our highest priced items, and so product mix does have some effect, but the overall conclusion doesn't change. We need some dramatic productivity improvements to stay in business. I've done some calculations, Andy. We need at least a 15% productivity increase in the next 3 months, and 30% by the next 6 months to be sure of keeping this business healthy and profitable. That means we need a production of 1,200,000 balls in three months and 1,380,000 within 6 months. Now, what I want to know is, are you the man for the job, or do I have to look outside?"

"Bill, whether it's me or someone else, I think you are asking the impossible."

"Nonsense, it's just your mindset. Remember Henry Ford: 'if you think you can, or if you think you can't, in both cases you're right'. Look, Andy, if it helps you, I 'll tell you this. I was talking with a couple of my golf mates and they tell me that they have achieved these types of results with the help of an external facilitator, a guy called Ralph Burton. Why don't you give them a call and get this guy Ralph's number? And we'll meet again in 3 day's time and you can tell me what your plan of attack is, ok?"

"Ok, Bill, you've got it," I say, hoping I sound more confident than I feel.

As soon as I get back to my office, the first thing I do is to ask my secretary, Catherine, to get hold of the friends of Bill from his golf club and to convene an emergency meeting with all the supervisors within one hour.

I speak with Bill's friends and listen to warm praise for the man and the company which had apparently helped bring about major productivity improvements in their own organizations, while at the same time improving the morale within the company and reducing the stress levels. They give me his contact details, and I get Catherine to call and fix a meeting for the earliest time available, which was next week.

I then ask Catherine for the latest complete set of production statistics.

Catherine is actually administrative assistant to the whole production department, and after 10 years at SportsBall is famous for ability to track down any information required quickly. She delivers first the figures for the Shaping and Stitching department, which are usually representative of how the other departments perform, and these are shown below:

SPORTS BALL INC PRODUCTIVITY STATISTICS
Stitching and Shaping Dept.

Indicator	Week Numbers					Month Total
	1	2	3	4	5	
Footballs	3,500	3,000	2,500	2,000	1,750	12,750
Volleyballs	4,000	3,500	4,500	4,500	4,200	20,700
Rugbyballs	2,300	1,800	3,000	3,000	3,000	13,100
Tennisballs	5,500	5,000	7,000	8,000	8,500	34,000
TOTAL BALLS	15,300	13,300	17,000	17,500	17,450	80,550
Number of people at work	25	25	26	26	25	24
Number of working days	5	4	5	5	5	
Man-Hours worked	1005	824	1045	1035	995	4904
Balls / manhour	15.2	16.1	16.3	16.9	17.5	16.4
% difference from average	-7.3%	-1.7%	-1.0%	2.9%	6.8%	

I notice that the weekly productivity figures vary by about 7% either side of the monthly average figure, and seem to rise from week one, which has the lowest ratio, to week five with the highest ratio. After checking the results for other months, and across other departments, it seems that this pattern of starting slow and finishing high is usually repeated Company-wide. The figures obviously vary, but the pattern is consistent across all departments. I further discover that there is no significant work-in-progress, that usually what is produced is normally sold within the same week.

One of the first questions which jumps out at me is: if this department is capable of producing at a productivity ratio of 17.5 balls/man-hour in a single week, then why they should not be able to produce at that level all the time?

This will be the starting point for my meeting with the supervisors. On time, they start arriving at my office. We adjourn to an adjacent meeting room, equipped with whiteboard and projectors. The team is complete today: there is Jimmy from Preparation, Jack from Cutting, Barry from Stitching & Shaping, Jon from Assembly, and Willy from Packing. I decide to get down to business straight away. After informing them of Bill's view of our productivity efforts, I explain to the supervisors that I have been perusing the most recent productivity figures, and then I ask them why, for example, the ratio of 17.5 balls/man-hour is not consistently maintained in Shaping and Stitching, nor the equivalent figures for the other areas. Talk about opening the floodgates! The next 15 minutes I listen to a barrage of emotional statements about how this productivity indicator is not reflecting what actually happens in the plant, how the productivity varies according to which products we are making, how the bonus system is unfair, etcetera. To be frank, I understand very little of what they are saying. They appear to be confused and disorganized in their arguments, sometimes contradicting each other.

Reminding them of the target that Bill has set us, I tell them that the minimum expected performance is now 17 balls per man-hour worked in Shaping and Stitching, which is a 4% increase on the monthly average of 16.3 balls per manhour. Each of their departments will also have to increase by the same percentage, and the corresponding figure for the plant as a whole will be a minimum acceptable 0.55 balls per manhour instead of the current 0.529. Again the outbursts. Barry splutters: "Impossible". Jon adds: "Can't be done without spending money on new machinery", and the others add their own comments in that same style. I let them work off their steam for a few minutes more, then I say: "I would like an analysis of why the performance is lower in the first weeks of the month and higher in the last. Please work on this for your individual areas and we will meet again in two day's time to review the analysis and talk about new productivity targets".

Two days later, we meet again. At the outset of the meeting, Barry informs me that the group have selected him to be their main spokesman. He tells me that they have met as a group, and have arrived at some conclusions that they want to present to me, and they want me to take these recommendations to Bill, if necessary, for rapid implementation. Barry continues: "We've reviewed the productivity targets, and as a group we supervisors are of the opinion that what Bill is asking for is not reasonable. The main problem is that the target of 17 balls/man-hour is too dependent on whether we make more or less tennis balls each week. This is because the tennis balls are the easiest and quickest to make. However, we think that it is possible to achieve the target he is asking for if we can find a subcontractor to make the footballs externally, leaving us with the possibility of using the workforce thus freed up to produce more tennis balls. As it is, because of a lack of capacity, SportsBall Inc. currently subcontracts out a production of 50,000 tennis balls per month over and above the 34,000 produced internally. According to our calculations, if we can subcontract instead the 12,750 footballs, we estimate that we can produce an additional 38,250 tennis balls with the same manpower, which would give a productivity ratio of 21.6 balls/ man-hour for the total month." Barry hands me a sheet with their calculations.

SPORTS BALL INC PRODUCTIVITY STATISTICS
Shaping and Stiching Department with supervisors' proposals

Indicator	Week Numbers					Month Total
	1	2	3	4	5	
Footballs	-	-	-	-	-	-
Volleyballs	4,000	3,500	4,500	4,500	4,200	20,700
Rugbyballs	2,300	1,800	3,000	3,000	3,000	13,100
Tennisballs	5,500	5,000	7,000	8,000	8,500	34,000
Extra tennisballs	*10,500*	*9,000*	*7,500*	*6,000*	*5,250*	*38,250*
Total tennisballs	*16,000*	*14,000*	*14,500*	*14,000*	*13,750*	*72,250*
TOTAL BALLS	22,300	19,300	22,000	21,500	20,950	106,050
Number of people at work	25	25	26	26	25	24
Number of working days	5	4	5	5	5	
Man-Hours worked	1005	824	1045	1035	995	4904
Balls / manhour	22.2	23.4	21.1	20.8	21.1	21.6
% difference from average	2.6%	8.3%	-2.6%	-3.9%	-2.6%	

Barry is now on a roll. He continues: "This would give a productivity increase of ….."

He stops in mid-sentence and goes to the whiteboard, waving the marker as if in some dramatic play. He writes in very large script:

21.6 balls per man-hour divided by the current monthly average of 16.4 balls per man-hour gives a 31.7 % increase !

Barry continues reciting what I guess are his now well-rehearsed lines. "…a staggering 32% rise in productivity!!" His grin is so wide it looks as if it is going to split his face open. I congratulate the team warmly on their efforts, and say that it is a privilege to be working with such a motivated group. Maybe I was a little bit too effusive in my praise, because they then spend the next 15 minutes pushing me hard to agree to implement their productivity improvement plan quickly. I suspect that the fact that they are on a productivity bonus scheme has something to do with this.

While this figure looks good, my 'gut feel' tells me it looks too good to be true. I just can't believe that I've been so lucky to find the solution to the 30 % productivity improvement problem in the week following Bill's ultimatum! The thought of subcontracting the footballs without a further analysis worries me slightly, for the simple reason that the margin on each football is higher than on any other product, and represents five times the profit achieved per tennis ball. This information had been kindly provided by the financial manager, Paul Bridges, during my meeting with him the previous day. At this point, I start wondering whether the number of balls produced is the best indicator for productivity measurement. I feel uneasy, and as my previous boss and mentor had always told me to listen to my instincts, even when my intellect tells me otherwise.

"Listen, team, it sounds great on paper here, but this is such a big step that before taking a decision, I must have some more analysis. A mistake here could be fatal to us all. What I'd like to see is how the weight of raw materials used in the process relates to the man-hours worked."

I can feel their groans, and I know from their mutters as they leave my office, that they're thinking that their new boss is a numbers and analysis freak. But we have agreed to meet again with the information I requested.

A few days later the supervisors duly report back showing the following table:

Productivity (kgs/ man-hour)

Material kgs	Weeks 1	2	3	4	5	Month Total
Rubber	50	55	100	90	30	325
Plastic	80	55	40	100	40	315
Cloth	30	55	70	80	20	255
Total Kgs	**160**	**165**	**210**	**270**	**90**	**895**
Man-hours	100	84	105	105	100	494
Kgs / Man-hour	1.6	1.96	2.0	2.57	0.9	**1.81**
% difference	*-11.6%*		*+10.5%*		*-50%*	
from average		*+8.3%*		*+42%*		

I look at these figures and instinctively scratch my head. It just doesn't make any sense to me. If these results are to be believed, then the plant is experiencing a productivity swing of 280% (taking the highest reported productivity of 2.57 kgs per man-hour and dividing it by the lowest productivity of 0,9 kgs per man-hour) in one month! Instinct and common sense tell me that this can not be so. I have already spent many hours walking around the factory, and my own observations during my daily plant tours tell me that people tend to work at much steadier paces than that! The only thing that I feel comfortable with concluding from this analysis, is that the weight of materials used is totally irrelevant to the calculation of the labour productivity levels of the plant!

That still leaves the problem of replying to the supervisors' request to subcontract the production of footballs. The supervisors obviously want something to be done earlier rather than later in the quarter, as it will have a greater impact on their quarterly productivity bonus calculation. Fearing that I will look indecisive and insecure in front of the supervisors if I delay too long on taking a decision, I say: "There's something bothering me about the proposal, and I want to study the question from a few other angles first".

But they aren't going to let me off the hook that lightly! They challenge me: "So what more information do you want to see?" I request to see figures showing the comparative production times involved in the manufacture of each ball type. After the predicted groans and surly comments, the supervisors agree to provide me with this data. I am left with the feeling that I can not postpone this decision too much longer if I want to maintain credibility with my people. As they troop out, I have the impression that Jon is whispering to Barry in a way designed to be just about audible enough for me to overhear their conversation, "You know what the trouble is? He just can't accept that we've come up with a better idea than he's had, and he's the University kid, not us!"

I hang back a few minutes. Can there be some truth in what he said (or at least what I think he said)? Am I jealous? Am I feeling so insecure that I want to hold back any good idea before I know how to present it to Bill so that I won't look too bad myself? Am I just too cautious? I honestly don't know the answers to these questions. At college, one thing they did not teach us was to spend time on self-evaluation. I decide that I must make a decision in the next meeting, and accept the benefits or consequences.

Two days later, the supervisors deliver the following figures to me:

STITCHING & SHAPING OBSERVED PERFORMANCES

Product	Machine time per unit	Crew	Man-hours per unit
Football	54 seconds	4 people	.06 man-hours
Volleyball	36 seconds	2 people	0.02 man-hours
Rugby ball	54 seconds	2 people	0.03 man-hours
Tennis ball	18 seconds	2 people	0.01 man-hour

Barry explains that the football takes 3 times longer than the tennis ball on the stitching machine, but as there are 4 people working on the machine when it is producing footballs, as opposed to two when it is producing tennis balls, the actual man-time taken is 6 times more for footballs, than for tennis balls. This information seems to stack up with what I already knew from my conversation with Paul Bridges, that the margins on footballs were 5 times higher than on tennis balls. Looking at these figures makes me think of the 'Standard Hour' concept, which I was briefly introduced to when I had studied Operations Management at university. I remember that the 'Standard Hour' is a term used to describe the expected amount of work that could be produced by a man in one hour at 100% efficiency, or at any other level of efficiency agreed by management and workers. I wonder if it would be a useful exercise to take the supervisors' figures of 'man-hours per unit' as a sort of rough-and-ready standard, and to apply them to the production figures we already have. So I close my office door, tell Catherine to hold my calls for the next couple of hours, and set to work. The table which follows shows the results of my calculations:

SPORTS BALL INC PRODUCTIVITY STATISTICS
Shaping and Stitching Department
using supervisors' standards

Indicator	Standard Manhours per ball	Week 1 Qty produced	Week 1 Standard Manhours	Week 2 Qty produced	Week 2 Standard Manhours	Week 3 Qty produced	Week 3 Standard Manhours	Week 4 Qty produced	Week 4 Standard Manhours	Week 5 Qty produced	Week 5 Standard Manhours	Month Total Qty produced	Month Total Standard Manhours
Footballs	0.06	3,500	210	3,000	180	2,500	150	2,000	120	1,750	105	12,750	765
Volleyballs	0.02	4,000	80	3,500	70	4,500	90	4,500	90	4,200	84	20,700	414
Rugbyballs	0.03	2,300	69	1,800	54	3,000	90	3,000	90	3,000	90	13,100	393
Tennisballs	0.01	5,500	55	5,000	50	7,000	70	8,000	80	8,500	85	34,000	340
Total balls & Std. Manhours		15,300	414	13,300	354	17,000	400	17,500	380	17,450	364	80,550	1,912
Number of people at work		25		25		26		26		25		24	
Number of working days		5		4		5		5		5			
Man-Hours worked		1,005		824		1,045		1,035		995		4,904	
Standard Manhours / manhour worked		0.41		0.43		0.38		0.37		0.37		0.39	
% difference from average		5.7%		10.2%		-1.8%		-5.8%		-6.2%			

Looking at these calculations, I see a different productivity picture emerging. Rather than productivity rising from week to week during the month, I discover that the productivity is rather constant in the first 2 weeks and the last 2 weeks of the month, and if anything it appears to *fall* towards month end, rather than rise. Furthermore, as the weekly variations in productivity are not too dramatic, I feel intuitively that this was a better reflection of the actual activity levels in the plant than the kgs / man-hour figures had implied. I start to get the sneaking feeling that if we had subcontracted out the footballs as requested by the supervisors and brought more of the tennis ball production in-house, that productivity would have possibly gone down, not up, as the supervisors had thought. To check these suspicions, I repeat the analysis with the figures suggested by the supervisors:

SPORTS BALL INC PRODUCTIVITY STATISTICS
Shaping and Stiching Department
using supervisors' standards and supervisors' proposals

Indicator	Standard Manhours per ball	Week 1 Qty produced	Week 1 Standard Manhours	Week 2 Qty produced	Week 2 Standard Manhours	Week 3 Qty produced	Week 3 Standard Manhours	Week 4 Qty produced	Week 4 Standard Manhours	Week 5 Qty produced	Week 5 Standard Manhours	Month Total Qty produced	Month Total Standard Manhours
Footballs	0.06	0	0	0	0	0	0	0	0	0	0	0	0
Volleyballs	0.02	4,000	80	3,500	70	4,500	90	4,500	90	4,200	84	20,700	414
Rugbyballs	0.03	2,300	69	1,800	54	3,000	90	3,000	90	3,000	90	13,100	393
Tennisballs	0.01	16,000	160	14,000	140	14,500	145	14,000	140	13,750	138	72,250	723
Total balls & Std. Manhours		22,300	309	19,300	264	22,000	325	21,500	320	20,950	312	106,050	1,530
Number of people at work		25		25		26		26		25		24	
Number of working days		5		4		5		5		5			
Man-Hours worked		1,905		824		1,045		1,035		995		4,904	
Standard Manhours / manhour worked		0.31		0.32		0.31		0.31		0.31		0.31	
% difference from average		-1.4%		2.7%		-0.3%		-0.9%		0.4%			

And sure enough, the results confirm my suspicions: making the change would actually be worse for the company, not better. According to these calculations, productivity would drop from 0.39 standard man-hours / man-hour to 0.31, representing a fall of *20%!* I start to see how sensitive the company's traditional productivity measure is to the mix of products. I have two immediate feelings about these findings. My first thought is to get the supervisors together and to bawl them out for pushing me to take an action, which not only would make productivity worse, but would probably also cost me my job! Then, as I am reaching for the telephone to call them to a stormy meeting with me, I stop myself in mid-air. Perhaps it is unfair to hold the supervisors accountable for this; after all they have been working for several years now with the balls/man-hour indicator, have gotten used to it, and are even paid bonuses according to it. I grudgingly decide that their behavior, although erroneous, was well intentioned, and was directly a result of trying to improve the indicator that the company used to measure their performance. The management system appears to be more to blame for the supervisors' behavior: if I really want them to change the way they look at management issues, I would have to change the information that they received. After all, I myself had given them a spurious assignment: to investigate why productivity starts off low each month and rises week by week. Based on what I now know, no such thing is taking place! At least something positive has come out of the red herring chase! My second feeling is: I need to get to the General Manager quick and renegotiate the productivity improvement targets he gave me, or at least get him to agree to a fairer indicator. Otherwise, I could conceivably increase productivity, but cause the company to lose money! And that's not the best way to start my career at SportsBall! After all, who wants share options in a company which is highly productive but is losing money? The question is: what productivity indicator will I propose to him? I don't know yet. Something inside tells me that I have not grasped the whole picture yet, and I feel very uneasy about asking Bill Braces for a meeting to renegotiate my productivity targets (or at least how they are measured!) until I know the questions that Bill would probably ask and what my replies should be. So, discretion being the better part of valor, I decide that it would be a good idea not to go to the General Manager just yet, until I have had time to work out and propose an alternative. I call Bill's secretary and ask to reschedule our meeting until after I've had a chance to interview Ralph Burton.

Chapter 2. Ensure you are measuring productivity correctly

The next day, as I walk into my office, I notice a photocopy of a newspaper article on my desk with a Post-It attached. The message is from Bill, and says that I would find the article interesting. I start reading: *"In any business, whether profit or non-profit, it is desirable and often essential to have an accurate and common unit of measure for the volume of work to be done, in order to plan and schedule and to be able to commit realistic delivery dates to customers. It is also highly desirable to have an accurate and common unit of measure for measuring the productivity of the resources used to produce that work. In many instances, this may mean two separate indicators."* God, I think, Bill must have been reading my mind, or maybe he's had my office bugged!

The article goes on to say: *"One of the things that can distort normal indicators of work volume and productivity is an inadequate indicator which does not take into account the effect of product mix. As a result of distortion caused by product mix, problems such as over or under crewing, hidden productivity loss and exaggerated productivity gain can occur. Even worse, this distortion can lead to the wrong decisions being taken."*

I stop to ponder that this so nearly happened with me. I was almost on the verge of agreeing to subcontract out the production of footballs, as a result of the supervisors' recommendations, which are based on an indicator which distorts the picture of what is actually happening. Had I done this, the result would actually have been to decrease productivity and to cause the Company to lose money! At this stage, the only conclusion I feel safe with is that the traditional measure of balls / man-hour is not only misleading but also potentially dangerous for the company's profitability! But I am unsure about what to propose as an alternative.

At the end of the article, I notice the name of the author. Ralph Burton. The very same guy who is due to visit me that afternoon! My reverie is broken by the phone. It's Bill Braces, inviting me to pop around to his office for a coffee and to chat about my productivity project and a new machine he is considering purchasing. It occurs to me that when Bill uses the word "invitation", he is merely being diplomatic; I know a summons when I hear one. My feeling is that he will try to get some updated information out of me before I am ready, and that my request to reschedule the review meeting with him would come to naught. "Oh well, can't avoid it forever. Probably better now than later", I mutter to myself, as I grab up my working papers on the productivity project and head out the door.

After a small amount of social conversation and an even smaller coffee, Bill broaches the subject. "I thought I should tell you Andy, that we have taken a decision to purchase a new line of stitching machinery, which is supposed to give us a 12 % productivity improvement. I wanted to discuss this with you, because I would like your 15 and 30 % targets to remain in place."

"Well, Bill," I begin, drawing a deep breath, "before going too far ahead on that, perhaps we should look at how we measure this whole productivity thing. I brought with me some figures I've being working on during the last few days."

Over the next ten minutes, I proceed to show Bill the conclusions of my work with the supervisors, and explain to him in a voice that I hope sounds more confident than I feel inside, that the company's traditional measure of productivity in balls per man-hour is misleading.

"The more I think about it, the more I come to the conclusion that the standard man-hour is our answer. It gives us 4 advantages which were not available with the traditional method of merely adding up the different types of balls, as far as I can see: (1) we can relate the production achieved to an "ideal" amount of hours required to achieve it, and thus calculate the productively objectively; (2) by analyzing the differences between the 'ideal' or standard, we can detect where the biggest opportunities lie; (3) we can use the machine standard data to plan ahead for machine capacity and check for bottlenecks; and (4) with the standard man-hour data, we can plan exactly how much manpower we would need to produce a given volume of balls at whatever mix Sales put to us."

To my surprise, Bill readily agrees. "I always felt that there was something missing from the measurement, but as it is a traditional comparative indicator in our industry, I have never really questioned it too much. But this just raises another question in my mind." Bill hands me a sheet of paper with the following written on it:

Manufacturer's data: Comparative machine speeds for new stitching line

Product	Machine time per unit (before)	Machine time per unit (after)	% increase production
Football	54 seconds	48 seconds	12.5%
Volleyball	36 seconds	32 seconds	12.5%
Rugby ball	54 seconds	48 seconds	12.5%
Tennis ball	18 seconds	16 seconds	12.5%

While I look over the sheet, Bill continues: "As you can see from these figures supplied by the manufacturer, the machine times per unit are faster. They claim that these improvements should give us 12 % more production for the same input. But you have put a doubt in my mind. This is my problem with what you've told me: I can measure and show this increase in productivity using 'balls per man-hour', but this productivity improvement will not show up if measured in 'standard hours per man-hour', because the increase in machine speeds reduces the amount of standard hours attributed to each ball."

"Can I use your computer a few minutes to check that out?" I ask Bill. Upon his ok, I proceeded to plug these figures into the spreadsheet which I'd conveniently brought on disk to the meeting. The following results came out:

UNITS PER HOUR *BEFORE* NEW MACHINE

Product	Mach. time / unit (seconds)	Crew	Man-hours per unit	Units per hour
Football	54	4	0.06	66.7
Volley	36	2	0.02	100
Rugby	54	2	0.03	66.7
Tennis	18	2	0.01	200

UNITS PER HOUR *AFTER* NEW MACHINE

Product	Mach. time / unit (seconds)	Crew	Man-hours per unit	Units per hour
Football	48	4	0.053	75
Volley	32	2	0.0178	112.5
Rugby	48	2	0.0256	75
Tennis	16	2	0.0089	225

"Yes" I agree, "I can see that whereas before 200 tennis balls could be produced with a team of 2 in an hour, now 225 will be produced. But in both cases, we are just producing 2 standard man-hours. Look:

before, 200 balls   x 0.01 man-hours per ball, gives 2 standard man-hours.

After, 225 balls x 0.0089 man-hours per ball also give 2 standard man-hours.

So, even though we are producing 12.5% more balls with the same workforce, it appears that there has been no productivity improvement. Something is wrong with this. This is something I'll bring up with Ralph Burton, who is coming in to see me this afternoon."

While on that topic, I query the issue of the cost of an external resource, and Bill reminds me: "You remember that when we interviewed, you asked me what resources were available to you to solve the productivity challenge. Maybe you remember my reply?"

"Sure, you said that I could have any resources within reason, even if it meant that I wanted you to come in yourself every night until 11 o'clock and on Sundays!"

"That's right. And if your friend Ralph can help you get the result without getting me away from my family time, then I consider that a reasonable use of a resource!" chuckled Bill.

So we agree to meet again on this subject in 2 weeks time, having decided not to move the 15 and 30% targets until the picture is clearer.

Chapter 3. Differentiate between standards for planning and standards for productivity measurement.

That afternoon, Ralph arrives at my office as arranged. After a welcoming coffee, I bring Ralph up to speed. I explain about the 15% target for productivity improvement in 3 months and 30% in 6 months. I go through the traditional SportsBall Inc. way of looking productivity based on man balls per man-hour, the supervisors' proposal to subcontract out the manufacture of footballs, our work in developing a standard measure (standard hours per man-hour worked), the imminent purchase of a machine which would give a 12.5% productivity improvement, and the problem that this created: the standard hour measurement did not take into account improvement which would be generated by the machine.

"I read your article this morning, Ralph. You said something about confusing planning standards with measurement standards. Is this what is happening here?"

"Yes it is," says Ralph. "But before I go into that, I would just like to congratulate for having got so far on your own. It is quite difficult when you are working on your own without someone experienced to bounce your ideas off."

"Thank you," I say. "But I think it would be useful if we were to agree how we should work together. I reckon I've got to be showing some improvement in 2 months at best here, or the old man, sorry, my boss, Bill Braces, will start looking for a new Production Manager. So I frankly want you to guide me through a process using the benefit of your experience. Second, I will give my guarantee that I will question you thoroughly every step of the way, and if there's something I don't understand, or can't see the logic of, I will not implement it just because you tell me so. At the end of the process, we can calmly look back and analyze the lessons learned, but ease up on the 'learning to learn' style for the moment, ok?"

"Whew, it's not often I get such a direct instruction on consultancy style from a client. But it's refreshing, and I agree that we'll do it your way until we see the need to change styles," returns Ralph.

Ralph continues. "What I'm going to ask you to do is to take the standards you have developed prior to the purchase of the new machine, and to create a separate database using these standards. I suggest what we do is *freeze* these standards; in other words, from here on in they will not change over time, but will remain constant. We will now have two sets of standards; one set which will be constantly updated, as Bill suggests, for example to incorporate the improved production times with the purchase of the new machine. The other set is the set which stays fixed in time. Now, to avoid confusion, we need to change the name of the frozen set. A useful name could be the 'Equivalent Units'. Let me explain this. It is often useful to relate all of the products to a single product. If, for example, it takes twice as long to produce a football than a rugby ball, then you could say that one Football equals two rugby balls, in terms of the time taken to produce each. In other words, you could make 2 rugby balls in the time it takes to make one Football. In the same way, one Football would be equal to three volleyball's, and six tennis balls. So, if we make our football the Equivalent Unit, and assign to it a factor of one, a volleyball will have a factor of one third (0.33), a rugby ball one half (0.5), and tennis balls one sixth (0.167). It is usually easier for the operators and people outside of Production to relate to this sort of Equivalent Unit, and if you use a productivity system to drive a bonus system, it is even more important for you to have units people can readily understand and measure."

"But there is another way of creating our Equivalent Unit," continues Ralph, "and it may be more appropriate in your case. You have to decide how you are going to get 30 % productivity improvement, but you don't have a system that tells you where those improvements are. You do however, have information which tells you that there is opportunity of at least 60 % in the business."

"Come again on that one, please" I stutter, "how can you say that there is 60 % opportunity here?"

Ralph picks up the sheet of paper showing the productivity calculations I had made for Shaping and Stitching, using the supervisors' standards. "You see here the way you calculated that the productivity is equivalent to 0.39 standard Man-hours per man-hour? If we assume that your standards are approximately correct, then the difference between 0.39 and 1.0, i.e. 0.61 tells us that there is at least 61 % Lost Time or Muda in the business."

"Come again on that one, too, please" I stutter again, "what is this 'moo-da'?"

"I think I need to explain a little more what I mean by the word 'Muda' and the phrase 'Lost Time'. Muda is a Japanese word which is used to describe all of those things, whether activities, processes, or events, which do not directly add value to the product or service for the client. Your people may be extremely busy, but what this result indicates is that only for 39 % of the time they are directly working on activities which add value to the product for the client. Let me help you grasp this by asking you a few questions, and making a few notes as we go along. What level of customer rejects do you currently produce?"

"Two percent on average," I reply. Ralph jots this down on a piece of paper. "What percentage of internal rejects, scrap or wastage is produced?" asks Ralph.

"Well, our total material yield (measured by the weight of the finished goods that we ship divided by the weight of the raw materials that we buy) is probably around eighty two percent, meaning that total material loss is in the region of 18 %. If you subtract the two percent customer rejects, you get approximately 16 % of what we call process loss. About 6 % of this is unavoidable, such as off cuts. The remainder is waste, scrap or rejects produced during the process." I reply. Ralph notes this down.

"What percentage of the available time is occupied by machine breakdowns?" asks Ralph. "Approximately 18 %," I reply. Again, Ralph makes a note.

"And what percentage of available time is taken up by product changeovers on the machines?" asks Ralph.

"It varies of course, according to the product mix during any given month, but I would say on average we're looking at about 20 %."

"And what percentage of the time would you say that your people have 'idle time', i.e. you walk around the plant floor, and you see that they are not actively working for whatever reason?" asks Ralph.

"Again, it varies, but I would say about 15% is acceptable."

Ralph writes something down on his pad, then spins it around to show me his notes:

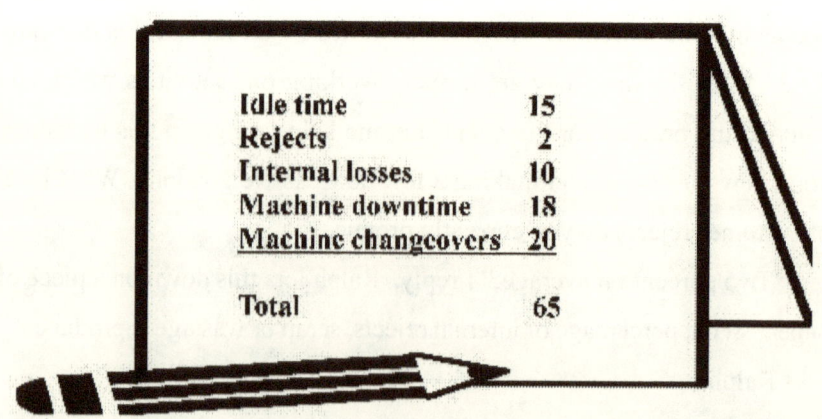

Idle time	15
Rejects	2
Internal losses	10
Machine downtime	18
Machine changeovers	20
Total	65

"You see Andy, just taking the major causes of Muda which you have described and adding up these approximate percentages, we get to the apparent conclusion that 65 % of total productive time is spent in Muda. I was looking to justify 61 %, and what probably happened here is that you're including some slack in changeovers and downtime, or there's some slack in the standards you are using. But it's close enough for starters."

I go suddenly quiet, and my face must have gone white. A full two minutes of silence must have passed. My God, what would Bill say of his new wonder Production Manager if he thought that there was 60% losses in the system? Would he believe in me or would he shoot the messenger? Finally I pull myself together and lamely say, "I just honestly can't believe that we are only working effectively for 40 % of the time."

"Don't worry," says Ralph, "this is quite a normal reaction. We will need to do a lot more work on Muda, but if I could just tell you now that the Japanese believe in their companies that only one activity out of 200 typically adds value to the customer. And, believe me, if this result is confirmed by further analysis, it will not be too different from anything which we typically see in many, many other companies. And also, please don't feel bad about this. This sort of thing is just not taught in universities. Rather than feel bad, about it, why don't you look at the other side of the coin? Why don't you decide instead to feel cheerful, that we are possibly looking at a way to increase productivity by 30 %?"

"I hope you're right, my job depends on it."

"But we're running far too quickly ahead of ourselves," says Ralph. "We still have not resolved the issue of how to measure productivity improvement. Do you agree on splitting up the work we have to do together into several discrete items? I suggest that the first thing we have to do is to establish a measurement of productivity which is meaningful. We should create a basic productivity measure using an Equivalent Unit appropriate for your business, and then set the base level, which is the average historical level of productivity, against which we will measure the 30% improvement we are looking for. The second thing which I suggest we could do then is to analyze the causes of Muda. The third thing which we can do is to draw up a series of action plans or implementation plans to eliminate or reduce the causes of Muda. The fourth thing we should do is to design some sort of management information system, which will give you this information on an ongoing and timely basis. Lastly, but probably most importantly, we should design some sort of production control system and training program for the machine operators and supervisors so that they can pick up and quantify the Muda on an ongoing basis. How does that sound as a plan of work?"

After plenty of questions, I agree that this sounds like a reasonable work plan. As I have some other meetings to attend, I suggest that Ralph could make full use of my computer while I was away, and that we would resume after lunch.

After lunch, Ralph shows some minor modifications he had made in my original spreadsheets. The first document shows exactly the same information as in my original spreadsheet, only that Ralph has reorganized it to separate out the standard hour calculations from the production volumes. Ralph tells me that it is easier to fit it onto a page this way. It's a matter of personal taste, I suppose, but it doesn't really matter to me which way he wants to present it.

SPORTS BALL INC PRODUCTIVITY STATISTICS
using supervisors' ORIGINAL standards with original volumes

Indicator	Std. Manhours per ball	Week 1	Week 2	Week 3	Week 4	Week 5	Month Total
		Qty produced	*Qty produced*	*Qty produced*	*Qty produced*	*Qty produced*	*Qty produced*
Footballs		3,500	3,000	2,500	2,000	1,750	12,750
Volleyballs		4,000	3,500	4,500	4,500	4,200	20,700
Rugbyballs		2,300	1,800	3,000	3,000	3,000	13,100
Tennisballs		5,500	5,000	7,000	8,000	8,500	34,000
Total balls		**15,300**	**13,300**	**17,000**	**17,500**	**17,450**	**80,550**
		Standard Manhours	*Standard Manhours*	*Standard Manhours*	*Standard Manhours*	*Standard Manhours*	*Standard Manhours*
Footballs	0.06	210	180	150	120	105	765
Volleyballs	0.02	80	70	90	90	84	414
Rugbyballs	0.03	69	54	90	90	90	393
Tennisballs	0.01	55	50	70	80	85	340
Total Std. Manhours		**414**	**354**	**400**	**380**	**364**	**1,912**
Number of people at work		25	25	26	26	25	24
Number of working days		5	4	5	5	5	
Man-Hours worked		1,005	824	1,045	1,035	995	4,904
Standard Manhours / manhour worked		**0.41**	**0.43**	**0.38**	**0.37**	**0.37**	**0.39**

In the second document, Ralph adapts the original productivity spreadsheet with the results that would be obtained with the new machine. It shows that even though production has increased by 12,5 %, labour productivity stays constant at 0.39 standard Man-hours per hour.

SPORTS BALL INC PRODUCTIVITY STATISTICS
using standards for NEW MACHINE with INCREASED volumes

Indicator	Std. Manhours per ball	Week Numbers 1	2	3	4	5	Month Total
		Qty produced	Qty produced	Qty produced	Qty produced	Qty produced	Qty produced
Footballs		3,938	3,375	2,813	2,250	1,969	14,344
Volleyballs		4,500	3,938	5,063	5,063	4,725	23,288
Rugbyballs		2,588	2,025	3,375	3,375	3,375	14,738
Tennisballs		6,188	5,625	7,875	9,000	9,563	38,250
Total balls		17,213	14,963	19,125	19,688	19,631	90,619
		Standard Manhours	Standard Manhours	Standard Manhours	Standard Manhours	Standard Manhours	Standard Manhours
Footballs	0.0530	209	179	149	119	104	760
Volleyballs	0.0178	80	70	90	90	84	415
Rugbyballs	0.0256	66	52	86	86	86	377
Tennisballs	0.0089	55	50	70	80	85	340
Total Std. Manhours		410	351	396	376	360	1,892
Number of people at work		25	25	26	26	25	24
Number of working days		5	4	5	5	5	
Man-Hours worked		1,005	824	1,045	1,035	995	4,904
Standard Manhours / manhour worked		0.41	0.43	0.38	0.36	0.36	0.39

Production volume increase 12,5%, but 0% productivity increase.

It seems logical. Production goes up by 12 ½ %, but the time per unit comes down correspondingly and the multiplied result is the same!

In the third document, Ralph uses the supervisors' original standards, but he has re-labeled them as 'Equivalent Unit Factors'. There is obviously no change in the result of 0,39 as a productivity ratio. He has merely changed the name of the units, not its values. Instead of 0,39 standard man-hours per man-hour, we now have 0,39 Equivalent Units per man-hour.

SPORTS BALL INC PRODUCTIVITY STATISTICS
using supervisors' original standards as *EQUIVALENT UNITS*

Indicator	Eus per ball	Week 1 Qty produced	Week 1 Equiv. Units	Week 2 Qty produced	Week 2 Equiv. Units	Week 3 Qty produced	Week 3 Equiv. Units	Week 4 Qty produced	Week 4 Equiv. Units	Week 5 Qty produced	Week 5 Equiv. Units	Month Total Qty produced	Month Total Equiv. Units
Footballs		3,500		3,000		2,500		2,000		1,750		12,750	
Volleyballs		4,000		3,500		4,500		4,500		4,200		20,700	
Rugbyballs		2,300		1,800		3,000		3,000		3,000		13,100	
Tennisballs		5,500		5,000		7,000		8,000		8,500		34,000	
Total balls		**15,300**		**13,300**		**17,000**		**17,500**		**17,450**		**80,550**	
Footballs	0.06		210		180		150		120		105		765
Volleyballs	0.02		80		70		90		90		84		414
Rugbyballs	0.03		69		54		90		90		90		393
Tennisballs	0.01		55		50		70		80		85		340
Total Equivalent Units			**414**		**354**		**400**		**380**		**364**		**1,912**
Number of people at work		25		25		26		26		25		24	
Number of working days		5		4		5		5		5			
Man-Hours worked		1,005		824		1,045		1,035		995		4,904	
Equivalent Units / manhour worked		**0.41**		**0.43**		**0.38**		**0.37**		**0.37**		**0.39**	

At this moment, I can't really see where he is driving at: it all seems a bit pedantic to me. But I'm a patient chap: I'll listen him out until the end. It is only when I see the fourth document that it all falls into place, and the dawn of understanding hits me.

In the fourth document, Ralph uses these relabeled Equivalent Units in a calculation with the volume increases due to the new machine. In this case, it clearly shows that a 12,5% volume increase leads to a 12.5% increase in labour productivity, as I would have expected, and as common sense would say!

SPORTS BALL INC PRODUCTIVITY STATISTICS
using EQUIVALENT UNITS with INCREASED volumes

Indicator	Eus per ball	Week 1 Qty produced	Week 1 Equiv. Units	Week 2 Qty produced	Week 2 Equiv. Units	Week 3 Qty produced	Week 3 Equiv. Units	Week 4 Qty produced	Week 4 Equiv. Units	Week 5 Qty produced	Week 5 Equiv. Units	Month Total Qty produced	Month Total Equiv. Units
Footballs		3,938		3,375		2,813		2,250		1,969		14,344	
Volleyballs		4,500		3,938		5,063		5,063		4,725		23,288	
Rugbyballs		2,588		2,025		3,375		3,375		3,375		14,738	
Tennisballs		6,188		5,625		7,875		9,000		9,563		38,250	
Total balls		**17,213**		**14,963**		**19,125**		**19,688**		**19,631**		**90,619**	
Footballs	0.06		236		203		169		135		118		861
Volleyballs	0.02		90		79		101		101		95		466
Rugbyballs	0.03		78		61		101		101		101		442
Tennisballs	0.01		62		56		79		90		96		383
Total Equivalent Units			**466**		**398**		**450**		**428**		**410**		**2,151**
Number of people at work			25		25		26		26		25		
Number of working days			5		4		5		5		5		24
Man-Hours worked			1,005		824		1,045		1,035		995		4,904
Equivalent Units / manhour worked			**0.46**		**0.48**		**0.43**		**0.41**		**0.41**		**0.44**

Production volume increase 12,5%, AND 12,5% productivity increase.

I decide to recap what I've seen so far, to make sure I've understood. "I think I can see clearly now what you meant by having one set of standards for planning, and another set of standards for recording productivity improvement. If I understand right, your argument is that we should use what I will call 'live' standards, which are continuously revised as advances in technology and processes happen, in order to plan and schedule through the production process. These standards can be what we have called our 'standard machine time' or 'standard man-time'. But in order to show improvements in productivity through management actions or through technological improvements from one year to another we need something else. One way to do this is to take the first set and to effectively 'freeze' these standards at some point in time and continuously refer back to these 'frozen standards' as a base. These frozen standards can be expressed in terms of a single product if we wish, and we refer to these frozen standards as 'Equivalent Units'. The purpose of these Equivalent Units is not to plan or schedule production, but to record productivity improvements against a historical base. Have I summed up correctly?"

"10 out of 10!" laughs Ralph.

Chapter 4: Know where the opportunities are

"So, now we know how to measure your factory's productivity in a fair and objective way, it seems as if all we have to do is to decide what needs to happen to get the 15% and 30% increases your boss Bill has asked of you, right?" Ralph asks me.

"That's about the size of it," I respond. "And we can discount the first suggestion that the supervisors came up with, subcontracting football production. Far from increasing productivity, that would have decreased it! And paid an undeserved productivity bonus to boot!"

"I think that the problem is that your supervisors have been focusing on the wrong things in their understandable desire to increase productivity," suggests Ralph. "Perhaps it would be useful if you were to get them all together, and I can give them a few hours training on the concepts of Muda, value added, and how looking at a business in this way can help identify dramatic productivity improvement opportunities."

"Yes, I think that would be an extremely useful idea, and not just for the supervisors; I intend to be there as well! I'll set it up for this Saturday morning!" I rejoin, somehow getting the impression that Saturday is not Ralph's ideal choice.

However, he doesn't voice any objections, and so Saturday morning finds the supervisors, Ralph and I in the large training room of SportsBall Inc. As we do not usually work weekend shifts, there is a strange air of silence around the plant, the only other people present in the plant being the security workers. Everyone is dressed in loose casual clothes, and chat in a relaxed manner, waiting for me to kick the session off.

"Good morning, everybody." I open. "I appreciate you all coming in on a Saturday. I know Jimmy had to make a special effort to reschedule his golf match. And Barry had a difficult negotiation with his wife, who wanted him to accompany her to the supermarket, and who said to him that he was only making up this meeting in order to avoid the shopping!" Some embarrassed laughs accompanied this statement. "The reason I've asked you all to come here today is so that we can pick Ralph's brains and experience for ideas about how we can get to our productivity targets this year. So, in keeping with the principles of good productivity, I'm not going to take up any more time and hand over to Ralph."

Ralph stands up and takes a position at the front alongside the overhead projector. "Good morning, everyone. As Saturday is probably not your first choice for a get-together, let's decide to make this an enjoyable and productive time together!", he begins. "This is the first of several sessions we are going to have together, as part of this productivity improvement drive. Today, we are going to cover some basic concepts: Muda and Value Added to the Client, or VAC for short."

"Muda is a very simple and useful Japanese word which means: *'any activity, process or operation which does not add value to the product or service for the customer or client.'*

Muda is waste of all kinds: it could be duplication, errors, rework, excess production, doing unnecessary activities, lost time etc. Later on during this session I'll hand out some lists of kinds of Muda for production and service activities.

The other side of the Muda coin is VAC (value added to the client). What is not Muda is VAC, and what is not VAC is Muda. If the sum total of an operation is 100%, a percentage is VAC and the remaining percentage is Muda. In a typical service or administration or production operation, you can normally show that only 10 % of what happens is VAC and the remaining 90 % is Muda.

I don't know how many of you have heard of José Antonio Lopez. He's the guy who made himself famous saving billions of dollars for General Motors, then was the subject of an acrimonious legal battle between GM and Volkswagen when he jumped ship to Volkswagen. After this experience he wrote a book called 'You Can!' In this book, he cites a study done in Japan where a group of companies were classified as good, regular and poor. In the good companies the study found that only one activity out of 200 actually adds value to the client! In the poor companies the comparative figure is one in a thousand. And this study was done when Japan was at the height of its productivity!

In understanding Muda, it is important to separate activity from productivity. If a man digs out a hole and then fills it in again, he may be very active, and very busy as can be seen by how much he is sweating. But if no one wants to buy this hole, if it does not add value to anyone's life, then his productivity is zero. No one has any use for a hole dug out and filled in again. No one will pay for it because it adds no value to anyone's life. This is true even for gravediggers; their client has already died!" Through his smile as he said this, we guessed that this was one of Ralph's little jokes.

"All too often in organizations we engage in activities which are for internal consumption: no customer is going to pay for them. An example: I worked in a large bank and witnessed the following. One day the bank President was walking down a corridor and happened to notice a door which was scratched and looking shoddy. He made an off-the-cuff comment about it. The workers nearby who heard the comment, interpreted it as instruction. They proceeded to leave what they were working on, which was a minor project designed to improve customer service, in order to organize the repairs for the door. And they did an excellent job. The repaired door was perfection in every detail. But meanwhile, customers were outside still waiting in long queues. It can be argued that the whole process of repairing that door was Muda."

After Ralph's opening speech, he invites the group to discuss for a while the concept of Muda, asking questions as needed. Then he shows a video illustrating a practical example of Muda in industry, where an activity which typically takes several months is completed in a matter of days! Following this, Ralph says: "Right now, you have an intellectual understanding of what Muda is. But it will never be a useful and powerful concept to you until you understand it here," *(thumping his stomach with his fist)* "and the only way to achieve that is to get you to experience it. So now we are going to do a practical exercise in living, quantifying and reducing Muda."

He then proceeds to split us up into two smaller groups, representing two competing companies. We have three production cycles, and at the conclusion are able to quantify for ourselves that we effectively started out with 90% Muda, even though no one had this appreciation at the start. When this exercise is completed, Ralph hands out two sets of documents, '**Examples of Muda in Production Areas**' and '**Examples of Muda in Administration Areas**', *(copies at the end of this Chapter)* asking the teams to identify which of these examples were prevalent in their own areas.

Twenty minutes later, the two teams report back, each one through a nominated spokesman. Both teams conclude that the majority of the examples listed are found in their own areas, as well as other types of Muda over and above those listed. "We want to get started right away drawing up action plans to eliminate these Mudas," they report.

"Great," replies Ralph, "but which ones are you going to tackle first, and in what order?"

"Well, surely we have to tackle all of them, so does it matter what order we do them in?" asks Barry, the supervisor who would have been queuing at a checkout at that time on a 'normal' Saturday.

"We are here today because we are seriously interested in increasing productivity, right?" asks Ralph. A general chorus of agreement. "Ok, so if we want to go about this in a productive way, wouldn't it make sense to solve those items which have the biggest impact first?" A muted chorus of agreement.

"I don't see that it really matters if we're going to end up solving them all anyway," voices Barry, to the accompaniment of quite a few nodding heads.

"Ok, it's time we spoke about the Pareto effect, also known as the 80-20 rule," says Ralph.

"Sorry, Ralph, but we're just plain engineering folk here. Do you mind speaking English?"

"Apologies, perhaps I should have told you what I was going to tell you before telling you," grins Ralph. "Pareto was an Italian 19th Century mathematician who discovered a strange but everyday effect that dominates every aspect of our lives. What he discovered was that 80% of the results of any process are usually generated by only 20% of the causes. For example, have you ever noticed that 80% of your sales are generated by 20% of your salesmen? That 80% of your sales are generated by 20% of your clients? That 80% of your inventories are generated by 20% of your products? That 80% of the wealth in this country is in the hands of 20% of the people? That 80% of the wear in your living room carpet happens over only 20% of its area? That 80% of your quality issues are generated by 20% of the problems? That in any party 80% of the jokes are told by 20% of the people present at the party? The examples go on and on. So, knowing this law, we can ask ourselves: *'what are the 20% of the causes*

on this list which will give us 80% of the benefit?' Because if we want to apply our own time productively, surely we want to do those things which will have the biggest impact in the shortest time?"

"Yes, of course we do," I jump in, to the supervisors' defence. "But we don't have that information. Are you saying that we should do nothing until we get that information, because that is a mammoth time-consuming task? Won't we be falling into the trap of 'paralysis by analysis', and losing time when we could be actively solving our problems?"

"Well, it depends on what you want," said Ralph. "If you want to tackle the problems now as a matter of urgency, then perhaps it would be wise to get some quick quantifications of these causes of Muda in order to prioritise their implementation. But if you decide that this is essential management information, which would allow you as a management team to always know where the losses are, and where you can dedicate your limited and expensive time to maximum effect, and you decide that you should have this information coming to you on an automatic and regular basis, then you should contemplate a different course of action. The question you should ask yourselves: do you want a quick fix, or do you want this information coming through regularly so that you don't have to go through other future emergency quick fixes?"

"Well, put like that, what obviously interests us the most is to have this information quantified on a regular and frequent basis. But if possible I'd like a quick fix as well. How do you suggest we do that?" queries Andy.

"That is a long topic for another session, and we've already spent many hours today. Let's meet up in your office on Monday, I'll go through with you what we need, and we can then schedule to get back together with the team here," suggests Ralph.

"Ok, Monday it is. Thanks for coming everyone; it was very interesting, useful, and dare I say it? It was fun! Thank you, Ralph." Thus I conclude our Saturday morning together.

Copies of documents distributed by Ralph are shown on the following 6 pages.

<u>Examples of Muda in Production areas</u> *Page 1 of 4*

1. Work areas with excess of personal.
2. Unbalanced production lines. An operation, a person, or a workgroup works at a faster or slower rate than others in the line.
3. Lack of work assignment. The worker finishes his work and has to go looking for the chargehand or supervisor to ask what he should do next.
4. Supervisors outside of their area and are not available when needed. Operators have to go looking for them.
5. Employees without appropriate training constantly interrupt their colleagues.
6. Appropriate tools not readily available.
7. Waiting for mould changes or adjustments; the operator is not trained to do this and the mechanic is not available or he has not been called..
8. Waiting for transfer of materials (to receive raw materials or to remove finished product).
9. Poorly configured work layout (lost time because the operator has to move from his work area to obtain raw materials, tools, etc.). The layout of the workplace requires more physical work (e.g. lifting, etc.) or more walking than strictly necessary to do the job.
10. Rework, reprocessing, waste, rejections and scrap. Although the employee seems to be working, his corrective efforts could have been avoided, therefore it should be considered lost time.
11. Use of sub-standard raw materials, often meaning that the machines have to run at slower speeds.

12. *Working on the wrong product (when the employee is working on a product not included in the production plans nor requested by a client).*

13. *Repetitive causes of machine downtime, not solved by Maintenance.*

14. *Manual override of automatic machine speeds (lowering speed).*

15. *Poor time discipline (leaving early, arriving late, etc.).*

16. *Wait at shift start to receive the day's assignment.*

17. *Quality problems: waste or rework or customer returns for lack of appropriate quality checks during the process itself.*

18. *Time lost waiting for quality checks by inspectors. Operators not qualified to take their own quality measures.*

19. *Slow response from Maintenance personnel, because they cannot be located or because there is no formal way of communicating that they are required.*

20. *No priorities set for the Maintenance department (working on less important machines to avoid criticism for lack of activity).*

21. *Poor scheduling of machines, causing excessive product changes (there is no grouping by family of products to minimize downtime).*

22. *Waiting for the Finished Goods Warehouse to withdraw the product from the Production areas, due to lack of suitable space at the appropriate time.*

23. *Errors in planning or work scheduling, in the sequence of work, mistaken numbers, operations, etc.*

Fintan William Bohan

24. Shortage of raw materials in inventory due to failure to place the correct purchase order or at the correct time.

25. Excessive distance traveled by the product in the production process (implies more space, transport time and inventory).

26. Planning of work facilities: too many people need to use the same area at the same time.

27. Lack of tools or poor programming of tools. A single tool, which is continuously used, is required at the same time by more than one person.

28. Wrong workteam size. Using a smaller team, or an inadequate team, causes slower production or more rejects.

29. Untidy or disorganized work area.

30. Temperatures too hot or too cold.

31. Unnecessary junk or lack of cleaning.

32. Parkinson's Law: work expands to fill time available. People or groups fill the allotted time with the exact quantity of work that they are assigned and often it is less than what they are capable of.

33. Little flexibility of employees. When a small specialized group finishes its work, leaving them available time, often they are not qualified or trained to do other jobs.

34. Little flexibility between departments. Poor systems for transferring people from one area to another when necessary. Often, a supervisor will create work in his own section instead of transferring the employee momentarily to another section that needs a person. This tendency is natural, since the workload could increase at any moment, and the transferred person would not be immediately available.

50

<u>*Examples of Muda in Production areas*</u>   <u>*Page 4 of 4*</u>

33. *Uncontrolled use of overtime. This happens when the supervisor doesn't plan the amount of overtime hours required to complete an assignment. For example, when someone gets paid overtime hours for "just a few more minutes" (or some hours) to finish a job, simply because he or she wanted to finish it, not because he or she had to finish it. Another problem with overtime is that the work rhythm is slower because the employee is tired, or because the supervisor has already left and a problem arises that the employee cannot solve.*

34. *Duplication of effort and of work.*

35. *Excessive or unproductive meetings.*

Examples of Muda in Administrative Areas   *Page 1 of 2*

1. *Many unnecessary stages in the processing of documents.*

2. *Excessive number of authorization signatures.*

3. *Culture of lack of trust.*

4. *Excessive distances traveled between work sections.*

5. *Lost time.*

6. *Excessive distribution of memos ("A/C memos"). Many, if not most memos are not written to inform their recipients or to add real value to the client in the delivery of his product or service. Such memos are written in order to 'document one's actions' so as to avoid recriminations or blame later on, We call this A/C memos where A/C means 'ass-covering'.*

7. *Unnecessary memos.*

8. *Information held up in peoples' in-trays.*

9. *Activities that don't add value for the client.*

10. *Rework.*

11. *Over-designed processes.*

12. *Excessive and / or unnecessary meetings.*

13. *Duplication of activities and information.*

14. *Unnecessary phone calls.*

15. *Not attending scheduled meetings: causes waiting for group decisions.*

Examples of Muda in Administrative Areas Page 2 of 2

16. Memo with unnecessary information.

17. Perfectionism: 'paralysis by analysis'.

18. Unnecessary correspondence.

19. Bad planning or lack of planning.

20. Little clarity of departmental objectives.

21. Non-coherent objectives among departments.

22. Disorder and untidiness (papers).

23. Distractions.

24. Interruptions to meetings.

25. Unexpected or unprogrammed visits.

26. Avoidable emergencies.

27. Bad work assignment.

28. Slow decision-making.

29. Little delegation: routine administrative work performed by expensive or over-qualified employees.

30. Inadequate communication.

31. Lack of methods, procedures or systems.

32. Lack of priorities: unimportant but urgent jobs done first.

33. Slowness of computer systems.

34. Bureaucracy.

35. Reading newspapers and magazines not related to the work to be done.

Chapter 5: The Treasure Hunt

If an industrial spy were observing me in my office the following Monday, he would have seen me deep in conversation with Ralph. I start by summing up progress to date:

"So far you've helped me to understand how to measure productivity improvements over time. Also, I am now clearer on the difference between a productivity measure and a planning or scheduling standard. And most recently, on Saturday morning in fact, you helped me clarify in my mind the difference between activities which add value to the client and activities which are 'Muda', i.e. they have no value for the client in the final product or service. I must admit that I was surprised and shocked when you told me that our productivity was at best 39%, and Muda was 61%. I've always thought that we have a high level of activity in the plant, as everyone appears to be constantly moving, and rarely standing idle. That's why I did not see that the productivity ratio we calculated of 0.39 standard man-hours per man-hour was an indication that there was approximately 60% Muda in the system. I just saw it as another ratio, just like balls per man-hour; I didn't feel that you could draw any other conclusion from the figure. Now, correct me if I am wrong in this, but is this like saying that I was confusing a high level of activity with a high level of productivity?"

Ralph thinks for a few moments, and then replies, "You know, I think that's a very good way of explaining it; confusing activity with productivity. I normally explain to participants in my training seminars that it's like digging a hole in the road to fill it in again later, like the old film clips of prisoners in forced labour camps. You may be working very hard, even sweating like a Turkish wrestler, but in terms of productivity, or value added for someone or something, the result is zero."

"Well, what are the next steps, then?" I ask.

"Firstly, I'd like to give you a little personal training session on productivity, so that at least you and I are singing off the same song-sheet. We now know our starting point for productivity, which is 0.39 Standard Hours per man-hour. Let's get used to saying 0.39 Equivalent Units per man-hour, because we're going to 'freeze' these standards at their values of today, and use the term standard man-hours from now on to refer to the most up-to-date and improved processes as they are introduced. So the set of standards which changes, as new processes are introduced, is called *'Standard Man-Hours'*, and the set of standards which is fixed in time we call the *'Equivalent Units'*. Are you okay with this concept?"

Seeing me nod my head, he continues: "Now, we know that we must generate a 30% improvement in excess of the improvement to be achieved by the purchase of the new machine. This means that:............"

Ralph stands up to make some calculations on the whiteboard.

"...a 30% increase on 0.39 gives you a ratio of 0.51, which you can see is 130% of 0.39... To get a further 12.5% means that we must take a ratio from 0.51 up to 0.57, which is 0.51 times 112.5%... That in turn means that, speaking in very rough terms, we need to reduce the Muda to 49 % or less".

"Let's tabulate these results, and I'll use 100 man-hours to make the calculations easier."

	Base	Target without MultiStitch	Target with MultiStitch
Equivalent Units	39	51	57
Man-hours	100	100	100
Productivity Ratio	0.39	0.51	0.57
Implied Muda	61%	49%	49%

"Hold on, Ralph," I interrupt. "I get the way you calculate implied Muda of 61 % and 49 %, but I don't understand why you leave it unchanged with the new machine. Shouldn't the implied Muda in the last column be 43 %, using the guideline you mentioned earlier on?"

"I can see why you say that; let me explain. The only meaningful way we have of measuring Muda is against some sort of standard or other. But what happens if that standard is slack, by which I mean that it already contains a certain level of Muda? If for example, our standards have on average a slack of 20 %, our original base ratio should be 0.31; can you see that?"

I take out my calculator and punch in the numbers 0.39 multiplied by 80 %. "Yes, I can," I affirm. "But why should there be slack in the standards?"

Ralph pauses to take a deep breath before replying. "Believe me, there always is. You'll never reach 100 % productivity. Please accept this as a fact. There are always opportunities to do better. Hence the well-known Japanese term 'kaizen', or 'continuous improvement'. As a former boss of mine used to say: 'the biggest room in the world is the room for improvement'. So we have a choice here: to place our yardstick in the ground somewhere and start working from that, or we wait and spend a lot of time analyzing until we can get as perfect a measure as possible before starting to measure improvement. Bearing in mind that we can always vary the standards at any time in the future to incorporate improvements in a matter of seconds using computer spreadsheets, and considering the time pressure we are working against, it really does not matter too much where we stick our starting productivity ratio, because we are interested primarily measuring improvements over time against it. It is quite feasible that at some point in the future you will report productivity ratios in excess of 1.0 (unless of course you reset the base, say every two years or so, like economists do from time to time to adjust the makeup of the standard basket of goods that they used to measure changes in inflation). So, in the interests of pragmatism and speed today, I suggest that we start with 0.39 as it represents the best information we have today. So long as we are comparing like with like, or apples with apples, it really does not matter too much where the base ratio comes out. But let's get back to your previous question. Why 49 % Muda after the MultiStitch machine goes in? Well, the way I see it is this -the MultiStitch is going to help us to produce more in the same time that we are actually producing, which is 39 % of the time right now, right? Remember that the standard hour per man-hour ratio we calculated when we adjusted the standards to take into account the improved MultiStitch times? The ratio still comes out at 0.39, because we produce more, but with less time for each unit. But all of the other factors which you listed for me, the other causes of Muda [*Ralph pulls out from his notepad the table prepared previously*] are not affected by the MultiStitch machine, correct?"

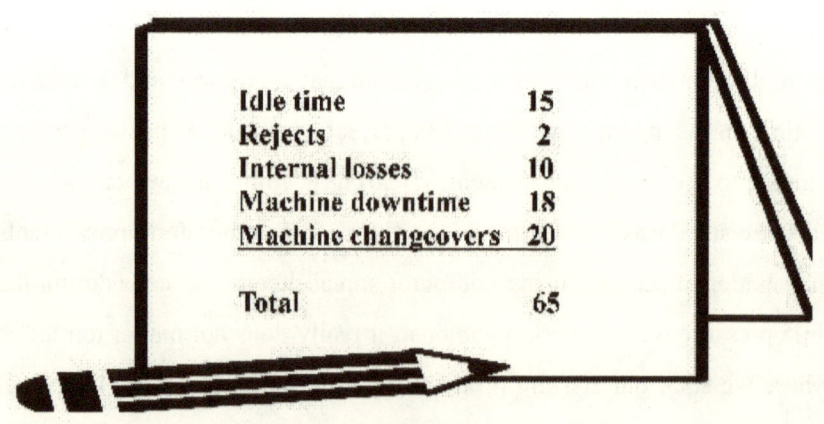

Idle time	15
Rejects	2
Internal losses	10
Machine downtime	18
Machine changeovers	20
Total	65

I suddenly feel relieved. "Yeah, I get it now. This looks like an argument for maintaining the productivity measure of standard hours per man-hour, because even when the standards change, it always gives you an idea of the amount of Muda in the system. But I agree with you that we need the Equivalent Unit in order to show improvements in productivity; however, do you think we should be using both?"

"Possibly, depending on the business. But the idea is valid. Another way of achieving the same effect is to have an indicator for machine utilization. At the end of the day, you choose whichever it is easier for your business to collect," replies Ralph.

"I feel that we've spun off at a tangent, because we got together today originally to talk about reducing Muda, and we've had long talk about productivity. Granted, it's been very useful for me. But I'm impatient. Is there any thing else we need to cover on the topic of productivity before moving on?" I ask.

"There are other topics we can cover, in particular the difference between what we call Gross productivity and Net productivity. But I think we can leave those for now, and come to them in time. Let's get started on Muda hunting. How about straight away?" retorts Ralph.

Overtaken by enthusiasm, I had forgotten that I have a regular monthly production planning meeting scheduled that day before lunch. And given the troublesome start to my relationship with Brian Rogers, the Sales Director, I didn't feel that it would be well received if I were to send a deputy to represent Production. So I apologize to Ralph for the confusion, inviting him to accompany me to the meeting, to see first hand how SportsBall Inc starts off its monthly planning process.

Several times during the meeting, I ask myself why I am invited to this meeting, and what the heck Ralph must be making of it all. The purpose of the meeting seems to be for Brian Rogers, the Sales Director to inform

Production (i.e. me) which products he plans to sell in the coming months, and what level inventories of each product he expects to be held to support sales. I feel that Rogers could just as easily send this information to me by e-mail, and at least save me the bother of an unpleasant hour. Rogers is scathing in his criticism of the recent performance of production: "by our estimates, we have lost some 20 % of sales because we didn't have the correct products in stock. On some product lines, we have more inventories than we can ever sell. And for other products, we never have the inventories to support our sales levels. Our reputation with the regular customers is getting worse- believe me this, it won't be much longer before we lose them."

Bill Braces intervenes: "Hold onto your shirt, Brian. Andy has started getting into the productivity issue, and I know that he will have our productivity up by 30 % within a few months. That means we will be able to produce more and give better customer service."

It seems now that Bill has lit Brian's fuse. "Customer Service?", he barks. "Hah! Don't get me started on customer service! According to our figures, last month we shipped only 83% of the orders within the time promised. And we only shipped 72% of the orders complete with all the items asked for. That means we have a pitifully low customer service figure of 60%!"

I'm thinking, uneasy in my seat with the embarrassment: "Can it really be that low? Maybe he's got his math wrong." But a quick stab on my calculator shows that at least his math is fine. 83% of 72% does give 60%, unfortunately. We measure customer service as the percentage of orders which are shipped complete and within the promised delivery time, and so Brian is right. But my thoughts are interrupted by his shouting like a lunatic.

"I'm telling you, Bill, as your Sales Director, that with a 60% customer service, we are losing sales. The only way to improve sales is to hold more stocks of at least our top selling lines."

Again Bill Braces feels called upon to intervene: "And as I've told you before, Brian, we don't have the capital to be able to hold the stocks you are asking for. The only way forward is to improve our productivity."

But that doesn't seem to satisfy Rogers: "Listen, it's no good saying to our customers that we've become more productive, or even have the best productivity in the industry. All they want is the products they asked for, and on time, and they don't really care how productive we are. We should be producing more for inventories to compensate for production inefficiencies."

I ask Rogers why he seems to think that improving productivity will not help to increase sales. He replies, as if he were talking to a child: "Yeah, you can improve productivity, but for the love of God, try to get Production to meet its Production Plan. Do you realize that Production are only complying with the requirements of the Monthly and Weekly Production Schedules to 66%? In other words, they are failing to produce 34% of what we want, and often they produce stuff we don't need?"

Bill asks me to comment on this last statement. I say: "The figure of 66% that Brian quotes as Production compliance to the Plan is unfortunately correct, but this is an integral part of the productivity problem we are working on."

Rogers seems to ignore me completely and insists again: "I mean, you can have the plant as productive as you want, but if we are producing the wrong products, the customers are not going to buy, and we'll still go out of business but we will have the satisfaction of saying that we went out of business productively."

The meeting ended quite acrimoniously with Rogers muttering under his breath: "I hope to God you guys in production can do something better this month."

After lunch, I make it back to my office, with the taste of the meeting still in the back of my mouth. I find Ralph seated at the computer, having just sent a print instruction to the printer. "I was going to ask how did it go, but maybe I shouldn't, with that expression on your face," comments Ralph with concern in his voice.

"No, don't worry about it. I'll tell you about it later on, when we get through the Muda topic. What have you been up to?"

"Making headway on this Muda issue," replies Ralph. "We know roughly the main causes of Muda from the work supplied by the supervisors, but we don't know how important each cause is yet. So the next step I'm going to suggest is an analysis of the areas and causes of Muda, which will end up with a set of specific implementation plans. Then I suggest we work on a control system which will allow you to ensure that the implementation plans are successful, and to identify in the future on a regular automatic basis where the Muda is coming from."

"Ok, sounds good, let's get started as soon as possible!" I echo.

"Great. However, I need to clarify one thing with you, Andy. During this process of Muda detection and reduction, I believe we should be involving the workforce. What is your company's attitude towards the workforce, what are industrial relations like, and how do you get on with your unions?" asks Ralph.

"Most of our workers have been here for many years, and many were recruited directly by Bill, the founder. The company tries to practice a policy of open communication with its workforce, and a productivity bonus system. Bill Braces considers many of the workforce to be personal friends, and often says in meetings that the workers are the real assets of the company. He says that machines decline in value, and in accountancy terms they are depreciated yearly to reflect this. But people are the only assets which increase in value over the years, as they acquire more knowledge, wisdom and experience. As a rule, Bill practices a no-layoff policy, and as you know a large proportion of our production is subcontracted out, so it is unlikely that there will be the shortage of production volume in this company which would require layoffs," I explain.

"I was hoping you would say something like that, and this is the type of company where I like working. We can get very powerful results in a short time through involving the workforce in this process of Muda detection and reduction. After all, they are the experts in the business. They live with the processes day in and day out, and have more to do with the finished product which the client receives than you or I ever will. And the question I have for you is: will Bill agree to give us a letter committing that the company will not layoff workers as a result of their involvement in a project with us?" asks Ralph.

"The honest truth is that I don't know with certainty, but I don't think that will be a problem as long as Bill understands why and what we're trying to do" I reply. "From what I've heard of him, Bill is very much the champion of employee training. He likes to get personally involved in most training programs, usually appearing in person to open them up. He also usually insists on some sort of presentation to him and the management team by the participants on the training program, to make sure that they have obtained value from the investment in training."

"He sounds like an excellent boss to work for," says Ralph.

"Sure, he is a very humane type. But don't be fooled into thinking he's a soft touch; just the contrary. He says that his ideal is to provide an agreeable place to work where people can grow and develop, and expect the company still to be strong in 15 to 20 years, with most of the same employees still working here. But he goes to great lengths to stress that this is not a company where 'black sheep' or 'sacred cows' are tolerated. For example, if we find we have an excess of people following the installation of the new MultiStitch machine, we won't fire those workers. We probably will do one or more of three things: bring back in-house some of the volume currently subcontracted out; or absorb with our own people some services currently supplied by external firms on our premises, like buildings maintenance, security, and some dispatch operations; or simply implement a hiring freeze. We have about 300 workers here, and an average turnover rate of about 5 %, which means about 15 people leave us each year, and others hired to fill those positions. So what we can do is to freeze hiring and train up the people who are no longer needed in one of the departments so that they can take up the vacant positions which become available elsewhere. It obviously requires more time and work than simply hiring someone with the experience you want off the street, but it pays off in increased employee morale," I explain.

"What do you mean by black sheep and sacred cows?" asks Ralph.

"Well for example, in my first week, five people were fired for stealing, black sheep without question, would you agree? But, for example, if I don't do the job I was hired to do (which in this case is to get a 30 % productivity increase) then I'll be classifying myself as a black sheep. And as there are no sacred cows here, even managers, that means I'll be filling out my resumé faster than you can say 'get me 20% more balls!' That's why I told you what I told you, about how I want you to work with me - faster!" I'm grinning as I say this.

"Do you feel that Bill is applying undue stress to you?" asks Ralph.

"No, because Bill said that I could employ whatever resources I needed to meet that target, even if it meant that I needed him to work every weekend with me for next three months and to midnight each night to reach the target. He made it clear that he would give me whatever support and help I felt I needed, but it was up to me to ask for help, not up to him to impose it. I've been here already 9 months, and while I've got to know the operation pretty well, the only real progress made was discovering that the existing measures of productivity were misleading. Hence, my friend, your presence with me here today!"

"Well, that makes the background absolutely clear: you have got a very fair and humane boss, there is a high degree of respect for the employees in this organization, and you've got to show progress towards achieving a 30 % productivity improvement, otherwise you can be looking elsewhere for a career."

"That sums it up. Let's talk about the first step you mentioned; analyzing the areas and causes of Muda," I suggest.

"Good. On the issue of identifying and reducing Muda, I propose three fronts of attack. Firstly, a production control system which identifies Muda automatically and encourages active supervision on behalf of the supervisors. Secondly, a series of performance improvement workshops with groups of 20 to 25 of your shop floor workers. I call these the 'Champions' Workshops', for reasons which I will cover shortly. And thirdly, detailed product flow and activity analyses to be carried out by the supervisors."

"Whew. Maybe it's that I'm still shell-shocked from the meeting I've just had, but I think you'll need to explain each of these steps for me in detail."

"With pleasure," smiles Ralph.

Chapter 6. Identify the opportunities when they occur, not afterwards when it is too late.

Ralph appears to have a gleam in his eyes as he paces up and down in my office, to and from the whiteboard. He looks somewhat like a cross between a University professor giving a lecture and, whenever he stops to place his hands on the back of his chair, a priest lecturing from his pulpit.

"There are 5 key elements to a productivity improvement project. These are:

1) **Productivity measurement**: the ability to measure productivity in meaningful terms for management control and action, not just in terms of some convenient ratio;

2) **Short interval scheduling systems;** the ability to detect potential problems as soon as possible and to effect corrective actions as soon as possible in order to minimize their negative impact; this element is linked to the following, which is:

3) **Active supervision / facilitators for people growth.** This is really two points in one. Firstly, the supervisor uses the short interval scheduling system to interact with his people in a positive constructive way, *assigning* tasks with allocated times, materials and quality standards, and perhaps most importantly, *following up* to ensure that the tasks are executed according to schedule. Secondly, he uses this information to detect where his people have weaknesses, so that he can provide the necessary training in order to help his people reach excellence.

4) **Management productivity information systems;** the ability to resume meaningful productivity information on a 1-2 page

report weekly for the General Manager, allowing him to rapidly identify areas falling out of plan;

5) **Loss (or Muda) detection and correction** through the involvement of the line experts, the workers."

On my whiteboard appears this table:

KEY PRODUCTIVITY PROJECT ELEMENTS

1. Productivity measurement
2. Short interval scheduling systems
3. Active supervision
4. Productivity Management information systems
5. Loss (or Muda) detection and reduction

"I think we've already discussed your first point, productivity measurement. Do we need to go any deeper today?" I ask.

"I don't think so," says Ralph. "You've got the basics. The rest of it we can talk about as and when the information starts to come out from the operations areas."

"So, to point 2, short interval scheduling. That sounds like consultant jargon to me. What does it mean to us honest simple working people?" I hate jargon, whether from computer people, finance people, lawyers or car salesmen, and I rarely lose an opportunity to express my sentiments on the matter when it presents itself.

"Sure thing. Right now, from what I've been told, I believe you measure production at the end of each shift, or at the end of each production run, is that correct?"

"Correct," I reply. "The key operators fill in a Job Sheet after each production lot, or at shift end, as you say, whichever comes first. Sometimes, they have to complete several during a shift, depending on how many product changes there have been on that line. In addition to recording production volumes produced, they make note of the time taken in changeovers, and for any other downtime that happens on the line".

"Well, first of all I'll give you a quick answer to your question, what does short interval scheduling mean, then I'll explain it in some depth taking some examples from your own production lines. If right now, you are measuring production on average, say 2 times a day, short interval scheduling means that we will increase that measurement frequency to maybe every hour or even half-hour, depending on what we judge the best frequency is to achieve the productivity improvements we require."

I obviously don't get it. "Ralph," I say, "do you expect me to believe that just by measuring more often we are going to get a 30% productivity improvement? That's a mighty big leap of faith you're asking of me, and if I'm totally honest with you, I have to say that I'm not buying it."

Ralph seems totally relaxed in the face of my cynicism. "Just imagine if you will that you're on an aircraft. The captain has his course set out before take-off, right? Now, once the craft is in the air, what percentage of the time do you imagine that it strays from its course?"

"I really have no idea, Ralph."

"Well, if you consider all the factors that come to play during a flight, the wind, the rain, turbulence, air traffic, human error, instrument error and whatever else, all of these things move the airplane slightly off its course in different directions so that *most of the time* the craft is not even on its original flight plan. How is it then that the pilot always (we hope!) reaches his destination? Well, during the flight at very frequent intervals the pilots get feedback constantly from their instruments, from air traffic control towers, from other planes and even sometimes from the position of the stars in the sky, and they are able to make adjustments constantly so that they can get back closer to the original flight plan. Imagine what would happen if they didn't do this at short intervals. Imagine that in a 10-hour flight, they were only able to check their position every 2 hours. Let me do a sketch for you."

Ralph draws this on his pad and shows it to me:

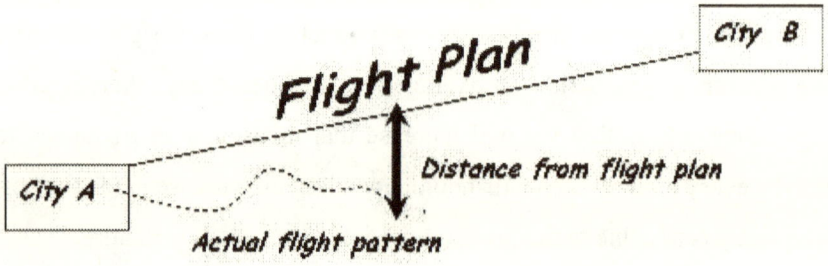

"The thick arrowed line represents the deviation from plan. For our purposes, if you want, you can call it the Muda of the flight. You can imagine the quantity of additional fuel that the captain must expend in order to cover the extra distance, without considering the fact that he probably has to fly faster to recover the lost time. And flying faster not only means even more fuel, but also places greater strain on the mechanical parts of the plane, meaning that its useful flying time between maintenance is reduced. All this without talking about the increased risk to his passengers' lives."

I'm not convinced. "Ralph, let's say I believe your proposal works for aircraft, but I just can't see it working in my production departments. Life here is just not that critical." Well, I did warn him at the start of our working relationship that I would not just accept everything he said to me.

The man must have a great deal of patience, because he still does not seem in the least bit disturbed by my apparent cynicism. After a few thoughtful moments, he says: "Andy, let's look at your most critical machine. What is it?"

"The Speedster 800".

"And what was last month's production on that machine?"

Looking at my reports, I find the figure. "276,500 balls".

"What does that represent as an average production per hour?"

Again I consult the data. " 3,788 balls per hour":

"What is the design speed of the manufacturer?"

I know that one without consulting any data; I know the design speeds of all my machines. "10,000 balls per hour according to the manufacturer."

"Are you saying to me, Andy, that your critical machine is only working at 38% of its design capacity?"

"Well, yes, but you'll never get 100%. And anyway, that figure of 10,000 is only a theoretical figure for perfect conditions in a perfect world. In real life, you get changeovers, which take up about 30% of the available time, you get machine breakdowns, ink quality problems, raw material quality problems, the time the machine is waiting for raw materials or design specifications or the production plans to arrive, waiting for the client to approve the design before running the whole batch, operator absenteeism, planned maintenance, the list goes on and on. And if we have no workload for that machine, which is fortunately not usually the case with us, we will not man it. Also the design speed varies according to the type of ball you are producing".

"Ok. Let's go one step at a time. What were the available hours last month?"

"Let's see. There were 21 days, the machine works one 8-hour shift, that gives 168 machine-hours available."

"And what were the downtime hours recorded on the job sheets?"

I hand Ralph the Production Report for the Speedster 800. It shows:

MONTHLY PRODUCTION STATISTICS SPEEDSTER 800

Hours available (manned)	**168**	**100%**
Setups	**52**	**31%**
Non-productive hours:		
Breakdowns	**6**	**4%**
Wait for customer	**4**	**2%**
Materials	**7**	**4%**
Planned maintenance	**6**	**4%**
Others	**20**	**12%**
Hours in production	**73**	**43%**
Total balls produced	**276,565**	
Production balls per hour worked	**3,788**	

"From this, it looks like the total lost time or Muda is 95 hours or 57%, right?"

"No, Ralph. You are counting setups as lost time, and that is not true. Setups are part of the productive process."

"I prefer to consider setups as a Muda, because they don't add value to the client."

"But how can you produce what the client wants if you don't changeover the machine to produce his product?"

"One way to eliminate setup or changeover time is to have that machine totally dedicated to one client or product. I recognize that this is not practical, but it would mean that setup time would be zero, wouldn't it? But let me finish my argument – *I know that you are itching to interrupt to argue against this notion* - by reminding you that once Toyota decided to consider setups as Muda, they set about looking for innovative ways to reduce it and in many instances managed to reduce their press changeover times by 75% and 80%. That would not have been possible under the old paradigm that setups are part of productive time. By the way, the same also applies to planned maintenance. Remember the aircraft analogy? Because our captain flew off course, meaning he had to fly quicker to recover lost ground, so to speak, the aircraft had to go into planned maintenance earlier than would otherwise have been the case, right? And while it is totally necessary, every minute in planned maintenance it is not *directly* satisfying a client need."

"Look, I'm not totally convinced, but ok, I'll accept it just for now. It all seems a bit academic anyway, how we label a thing. I will accept for the sake of argument that the total opportunity or Muda is 57%, but by no means do I believe that we can recover all of that 57%."

"Neither do I. But I want to be absolutely clear with you on what is Muda and what is not. Only as a second step will we look at ways to reduce it, but for the moment let us stick to the task in hand, identifying Muda through a short interval scheduling system. Anyway, the real point I wanted to make is that I suspect that the total Muda is greater than the 95 hours shown here. But we need to take a stroll around the production area before going further into that. Let's go, shall we?"

Now I'm not sure how to take this guy. But I keep my doubts to myself for the time being, and we head for the Speedster machine shop, where there should be 8 machines working, or I will be embarrassed. We stop at each machine, and Ralph engages each of the operators in conversation, making some notes from time to time.

Upon our return to my office, Ralph says: "Ok, let's tabulate what we've just seen", and proceeds to the whiteboard. My curiosity is piqued. Ralph writes:

Machine No.	Product	Speed observed	Ideal Manufacturer Speed
1	football	8,200	10,000
2	soccer	7,600	10,000
3	rugby	6,000	7,500
4	tennis	6,200	7,000
5	tennis	8,000	8,000
6	football	4,500	6,000
7	basket	3,000	6,000
8	volley	4,200	5,000

"I asked each machine operator why the machine was running below design speed, if that was the case. These are the reasons they gave me." I have two whiteboards in my office, something I inherited from my predecessor. Ralph goes to the second whiteboard and writes:

Machine	Reason given
1	Particles on material
2	Ink contaminated
3	Printer roller wobbling
4	No work planned to follow, slow down to stretch out till shift end
5	No variance to explain
6	No work planned to follow
7	Operator did not know machine could run at design speed
8	Ahead of plan by 2 hours, slow down to stretch out till shift end

"I asked the operators if they reported these differences as lost time on the job sheets, and their answers were: 'I don't have time to write down the small ones, just the big ones'; 'I write it down on the job sheet, but with so many things going on, sometimes I remember, sometimes I forget'; 'I did it once and the supervisor told me not to report that because they'd only bawl him out for it'; and others of the same style".

I must admit that at this point it is taking all my strength of will not to lose my temper and explode. How could my people say things like that? Especially to an outsider? If I understand this right, the operators are saying that they deliberately do not report all of the lost time causes. I say to Ralph, clenching my teeth, "this is making my blood boil. I've got a good mind to go back down to the floor and let them know my mind, and maybe roll a few heads too!"

Ralph says, "That would be precisely the worst thing that you can do and would destroy this productivity improvement project in an instant. You cannot blame your people for behaving in a way that is dictated by their management system. Rather than bawling them out, I think you should congratulate your people on their high level of honesty and professionalism".

"Ralph, you've lost me yet again, I'm afraid to say, please explain what you've just said?"

Ralph goes again to the whiteboard, rubs out his previous material (*note to self: get rid of at least one of those damn things from my office!*) and draws the following:

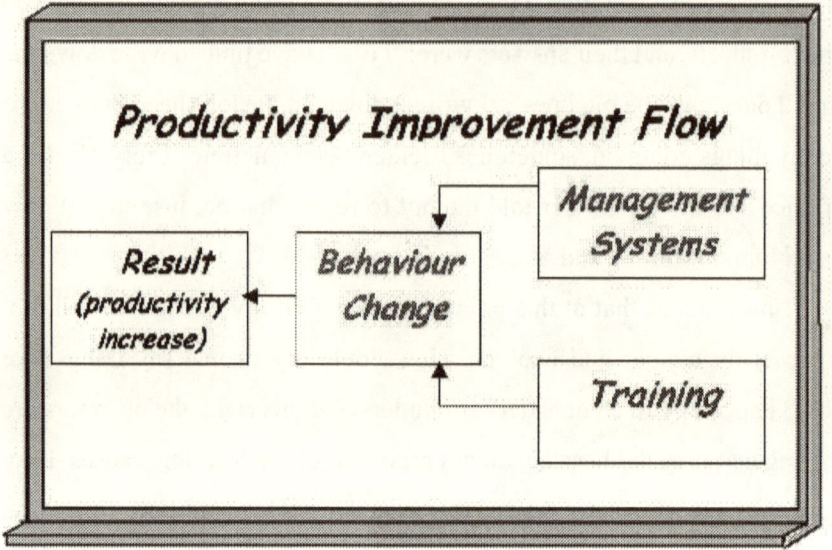

"You want to improve productivity, right? Well, your people are basically pointing in the right direction. Right now we have a certain productivity result. From memory, if we take the Shaping and Stitching Department as representative of the whole, then our starting productivity level is 39%, are you with me on this? And this is the result we want to change. A 15% increase means that we should bring it up to almost 45%, and a 30% increase means that we should bring it up to almost 51%."

He scribbles on the whiteboard:

39% x 1.15 = 44.85%
39% x 1.3 = 50,7%

"Perhaps you are wondering why these numbers still seem apparently low. As you said earlier, it is important not to confuse activity with productivity: you can observe that a certain person is very active, running from one task to another, but this doesn't mean that he is being productive. When we visited the plant, did you notice how often people seem to have to walk from one area to another, without any product or any visible value being added to the product? If the observed activity doesn't add any value for the client or the company, you should consider that that activity doesn't contribute anything to productivity. Therefore, it is not surprising if the first productivity evaluation is lower than you would have expected."

I ask Ralph to please expand.

"The productivity result we have today is because everybody in this organization behaves in a certain way. And the way they behave is in turn greatly influenced by the systems which are used to plan, measure, control and report on their performance, and their understanding and level of training in these systems. Your supervisors, for example, behave in the way they do, because that is how the system encourages them to behave, and that is how they have been trained to make the system work. Need I remind you how they were so keen to subcontract, something which they were proposing with the best of intentions, but which would potentially have bankrupted the company?"

"I stopped myself from bawling them out that day, precisely because I realized that: they were only responding to the way we, as Management, had set things up for them," I answer, somewhat cooler now.

Ralph continues: "As you say, they were simply responding to the measurement system which had been imposed on them. Often, this style of behavior is something that has been inherited from people who worked in the Company many years ago, and we keep still keep on working the same way because it never strikes us to question ourselves and find out how we can do things in a different and better way. In a sense, we 'can't see the wood for the trees'. Another example: your workers do not report all the lost time causes that exist, because somewhere in the past they have been told or trained not to bother with the small things, and only focus on the big ones. Again, like the supervisors, they are only responding to the requirements of the current system, and to their training on how to operate it. Can you accept that?"

"Now that you express it like that, I can. Thank you for opening my eyes. You said earlier on that you thought the real lost time was higher. How much do you think it is?"

"I think that there is another 9 hours of lost time in the system somewhere, which comes to just over 5%. What this means is that the figure you use for machine utilization of 43% is actually overstated; a more accurate figure would be 38%. And I think that the main reasons for the difference is that some of the lost time causes simply are not reported, because the operators will forget by the end of the day. Also, when the machines are actually producing, the operators are sometimes running the machines at slower than the design speeds because of various factors such as problems with quality of raw materials, lack of work to follow, which means that they stretch the work out to keep busy until the next lot of planned work arrives. These types of behaviour are not because the operators are trying to hide anything from you. On the contrary, they are simply the result of the way the current measurement systems are set up".

Ralph goes on; it seems there's no stopping him when he gets going. "To produce a result different to today's result, it is obvious that it is necessary to change something. Among the options that we can study are: changing the technology of the company by acquiring new computer equipment or new machinery, an option Bill is already following; or change the way that we manage the company; in other words, generate a behavior change through changing what we plan, control and report on. So it becomes clear that if we want to generate a different result without capital expenditure, we need to generate a different type of behavior, through providing different types of systems of planning, measuring, controlling and reporting the activities your people do, and then through training them in the best use of these new systems.

Now, I am not here to make positive or negative evaluations with respect to the personnel of the company, for these reasons: my belief is that the behavior of a person is strongly influenced by the management systems that in one way or another plan, control and report on their performance, be it subjectively or objectively. The other strong influence is the training that the person has received in the use of the systems and his or her consequent understanding of the systems. So, *if a relatively low level of productivity is detected, and if we also detect weaknesses in the management system for measuring, controlling and reporting productivity, and if it is found that the people have not been adequately trained in the understanding and the use of the tools of productivity, then it would be an injustice to negatively evaluate these persons for their apparent underperformance. To be fair, you must first of all correct the weaknesses in the management systems of measurement and control of productivity and then train the relevant persons in the understanding and proper use of these systems: Only then, if you observe that the person is not using the tools correctly, can you in all fairness conclude that the person is not correct for the company.*

If you look at it this way, it becomes clear that the responsibility to provide the appropriate tools (the systems and the training) falls on Management. So, if you were to go out now to let off steam on the shop floor about how the operators are 'lying', I guarantee that you will destroy any possibility you have of getting them to change their behavior to one which is more conducive to a high level of productivity".

"Ok, Ralph, I've cooled down now, and I promise that I won't bite anyone's head off. But at some point I must communicate all of this to my people. How and when do you suggest I go about this?"

"Step by step, my friend. First step A, then step B, and so on. With you, I am taking the opportunity to jump from A to Z in one bound. It's basically what you asked me to do. And in your position of management, you should be able to see the whole picture objectively and dispassionately. But it would be explosive if we were to do that with your people. What do you think will be the reaction if we were to go onto the shopfloor and tell your workers and supervisors straight out, without prior preparation and training, that they are only working at 40% productivity levels? And furthermore, that they are distorting the management information you receive, what are the chances that they will say: 'that's fantastic! I wish someone had said that to me before'? And, after bawling them out like this, what do you think are the probabilities that they will want to work with us enthusiastically over the next few weeks and months to improve the situation? Don't you think that their first reaction will be to think that they are going to be fired, and that they had better just shut up in the future?"

I inhale deeply before answering. "Yes, I do believe you're right. Blowing my top would make me feel good for a few moments, giving vent to my frustration, but it would cause long term damage to the good relations with my people which I've built up over the last 9 months. The potential damage would take months, if not years, to recover."

"You're exactly right. What we need to do is to communicate step by step, from A to B, B to C, and so on, so that by the time we get to step M, they can already see the light at the end of the tunnel. At that point, they should be coming to you, saying 'Hey, boss, we've just realized that we must be only working at 40% productivity, and we'd like to talk with you about how we'd like to improve it'. When this happens, you will know that you have succeeded; they do not feel threatened, but an important part of the improvement process."

"Right, let's get moving on the first few steps. What do you suggest?" I ask Ralph.

"I suggest that a general communication to everybody is step A, preferably by yourself directly to groups of a convenient and manageable size. The communication should cover…"

Ralph makes another empty space on my whiteboard, and writes:

Communications: Points for consideration

1. What is happening in the industry
2. Need for productivity improvements
3. Participation of everyone
4. No layoffs
5. New Production Control and reporting system
6. Champions' Workshops
7. Next meeting

"Why no layoffs, your point 4? Not that it should be a problem for us, because we farm out a huge chunk of work that we could bring back in-house. I would just like to understand the reasoning behind your request.," I ask.

"Because the machine operators are going to be a crucial part of the short interval scheduling system and the productivity improvement programme. If they feel threatened, then you can guarantee that their participation will only be half-hearted, at best. If we find that there genuinely is an excess of staff, and it becomes necessary to reduce the numbers of people, even after bringing the subcontracted work back in-house, then what we can do is to impose a hiring freeze. Nobody can be recruited from outside to fill any position which becomes vacant; we will identify the best candidate in-house from those whose positions are no longer required, and give them the appropriate training Over time, the natural turnover rate will bring us down to the required numbers."

"Fine. Understood. What is this new production control system, point 5 on your list?"

"This is a method I'm proposing to replace the current Job Sheet system. Let me draw up an example for the Speedster 800, the machine which makes footballs at a design speed of 10,000 units per hour".

Ralph sketches out an outline of a document in his notepad, and then passes the pad across to me. This is what I see:

SPEEDSTER 800 PRODUCTION CONTROL SHEET

Product		8 a.m.–9 a.m.	9 a.m.–10 a.m.	10 a.m.–11 a.m.	etcetera
Toolkit code XYZ123	PLAN	10,000	10,000	10,000	
	ACTUAL	5,000	8,000		
	VARIANCE	5,000	2,000		
	Lost Mins	30	12		

LOST TIME ANALYSIS BY CAUSE

setups		6	5			
Material shortage						
Material quality		12				
wastage						
Mechanical breakdown		5	5			
Electrical breakdown						
Machine failure						
Waiting customer		8	7			
Waiting plan						
No workload						
Operator cause						
electra						

"I reckon you'd better explain this to me, Ralph"

"Sure. You remember that you told me that the maximum running speed of the Speedster 800 is 10,000 balls per hour, which is the design speed. Well, simply put, I suggest that we compare our actual production each and every hour to the maximum feasible, and explain any shortfall".

This proposal gives me a very uneasy feeling. I can just imagine the reactions of the Unions. Is this guy here working for the competition and is he trying to cause a strike here? "Ralph, you know, it is difficult to take this idea seriously. It's a very harsh analysis; you're asking us to compare ourselves hour after hour to something which we both know is impossible to achieve, except for rare exceptions".

"Andy, please do not get me wrong. I am not asking you to achieve the maximum of 10,000 every hour. I know that to achieve the 10,000 each hour you would need to have absolutely perfect conditions for each and every hour, and that is *never* going to be the case. I am simply asking for the difference between what we actually achieve and the maximum possible to be quantified and explained. Let me show you an example. In the first hour of the shift, we had a production of 5,000 balls. Therefore the lost production or variance was 5,000. Can you see that this represents 30 minutes lost? The calculation could not be simpler. Look."

Ralph shows the following calculation on his pad.

- **5,000 lost units divided by an ideal production of 10,000 per hour = 50% lost in the hour.**
- **60 minutes in the hour (no tea or lunch breaks during this hour)**
- **50% x 60 minutes available = 30 minutes lost.**

"These thirty minutes represent the total Muda in that hour. Now, under the current system, these losses are not picked up automatically.

It is up to the operator at the end of the shift or the end of the job card to remember as best he can and to fill in the information retrospectively. This method, on the other hand, provides an objective external source against which he can measure and report the lost time as it happens, not after it is too late. Look again at this example. The operator knows that at 9 a.m. his production is 5,000 units, and can calculate what that represents in lost time. He calculates 30 minutes, and then he simply explains where those 30 minutes went. In this example, he reports that 5 were spent on a setup, 8 waiting for the customer to come to approve the initial production run, 5 on a mechanical breakdown and 12 due to material quality problems".

"Where does the supervisor fit into this scheme of things?" I ask.

"Good question. So what does the supervisor do? Well, right now he has 8 machines to look after, he always has 25 things waiting on his list of things to do, and obviously cannot do everything at once. How does he select what is the best thing to do at any given moment? It should be that action which has the greatest impact, don't you agree? Well, how does he know which of the possible actions he can dedicate himself to will have the greatest impact? Today, he relies on guesswork. Given the company culture today, we think that if he seems to be constantly busy, then he must be doing a good job. Better still if he looks stressed and overworked, then he's definitely doing a good job. But how do we know if he is really taking the actions that count? We don't, is the short answer. Let us suppose now that we change his behavioural pattern. Let us suppose that with the short interval scheduling system in place, our supervisor takes a tour of his area every hour. He has 8 machines to visit. He spends no more than a minute at each. At each, he asks: 'how much was the lost time? For what reasons? How much lost time for each reason? ' At the end of his tour, he examines his list for the machine with the biggest variation between Plan and Actual, he looks to see what was the biggest lost time cause at that machine in that hour, and he knows that this is the problem he must attack. He then proceeds straight away to take whatever action is necessary to reduce or eliminate that problem. It may take him 5 minutes or it may take him an hour, but he is sure that he is tackling the biggest problem and its solution will have a bigger impact than anything else he might do. At the end of the day, even if he has only acted on 8 problems, the solution to those 8 problems will probably have more impact than the total of the 25 problems he typically works on during a normal day right now. He will be able to leave the plant in the evening with a greater sense of satisfaction of having worked on what was really important, rather than leave stressed and worried about all the items which he failed to complete and which are still on his list of things to do for the following day. This is a practical application of the "Pareto Effect" in the working environment".

"To refresh my memory, Ralph, this Pareto Effect is the '80-20 rule' we talked about the other day?"

"That's the one, Andy. We will need to train the supervisors and the operators in the use of this tool. Can we organize small training sessions with the people, in groups of up to ten at a time?"

"Sure thing. We'll start with the first group tomorrow at 9 a.m., and I'll schedule everybody over the next 2 weeks. Let's meet again tomorrow for the first session".

The next day, Ralph and I meet with Jack, the Scottish supervisor from the Speedster machine area, and 10 of his workers, in the small meeting room adjacent to my office. I get the feeling that this should be a very interesting meeting. These guys have been using the Job Sheet system for at least 15 years now, and are not going to accept anything else easily. After introducing Ralph to those who had not already met him, I leave him to it. He starts off by explaining the need to control Muda as a means to improve productivity, and quickly enters into the presentation of his suggested format to replace our Job Sheet. I can see the operators visibly resisting, crossing their arms, leaning back and looking critical. Obviously, they are thinking that this means they have to register their production every hour. One of the operators, Micheal, happens to be the Union representative. I can see what he's thinking, is this a management trick to reduce employee numbers? I decide to interrupt Ralph's presentation to kill this one straight off.

"Sorry to interrupt, Ralph, but I would just like to clear something up for the guys before you go too far into your presentation. Team, I want to inform you that Ralph asked as a condition of working with us to help us increase our productivity, that we guarantee that as a company we will not use any initiative that results from his work here to lay people off. And Bill was happy to provide that guarantee. So please lend Ralph your full attention, and ask as many questions as you need. Please continue, Ralph".

Ralph shows a transparency which says:

BENEFITS OF THE PRODUCTION SCHEDULE CONTROL

- Live analysis of lost production units during each working hour;
- An explanation every hour for these production losses;
- Provides the supervisor with a tool to help him or her to prioritize his or her corrective actions every hour as a function of what will achieve the most impact;
- Quick, direct and objective feedback of performance to the machine operator;
- Ability to quickly detect anomalies in production standards.

The first question to come up is: "So, is the planning department now going to plan on us achieving 100% every hour and every day? Because if it is, then I can tell you for nothing that this won't work.."

Ralph replies: "That's a good question, but don't get too worried. What Planning will plan for will probably be something like this:"

He goes to the whiteboard and writes:

Planning Example

Plan Volume	= 100,000 balls
Ideal machine speed	= 10,000 balls / hour
Machine hours required at 100% efficiency	= 10.0 machine-hrs
Machine hours required at 60% efficiency	= 16.7 machine-hrs
Set up time planned	= 2.5 hours
TOTAL MACHINE TIME PLANNED	= 19.2 machine-hrs

"It is very important to understand that the use of this Production Schedule is NOT about trying to get you to produce 100,000 balls in 10 hours. What it is for is to help us identify all the reasons which STOP us from achieving it."

Michael asks: "Isn't that like information overkill? Won't we fall into the trap of paralysis through analysis?" *Good* question, I'm thinking!

Ralph appears relaxed though. "Right now, you guys and the supervisors are running around like beavers trying to tackle all of the lost time causes, right? But you don't know if you are working on the most important issues or not. You may be very busy, but that does not mean that you are necessarily productive." And Ralph explains the Pareto Effect / 80-20 rule again. I'm thinking he should just tape it and play the tape every time the question comes up. Say, that's a brilliant idea: and he's supposed to be the productivity consultant!

Carl, one of the machine operators, speaks up: "This is not practical, because it will be impossible to hit 10,000. There are many, many reasons why I have to stop the machine or slow it down. For example, I have to stop the machines a few minutes every hour to clean the rollers, to clean the blades, to check the gauge, and so on."

"Ok, let's take the first thing you said as an example. You stop the machines to clean the rollers every hour. How long do you stop the machine for, every hour, because of this?"

"I'd say about 4 to 5 minutes," said Carl.

"Ok. Now, why do you clean the rollers?"

"Because they get dirty, of course. I wouldn't clean them if they weren't dirty, now would I?" says Carl, to the accompaniment of general laughter.

"Fair point. What I should have asked was; what causes the rollers to get dirty?"

Carl replies: "it could be the ink quality, or sometimes the leather quality."

"Which is the most frequent cause?"

"Well, I'd say that 9 times out of ten it's the ink. We rarely get leather problems"

Ralph pauses and sketches on the whiteboard:

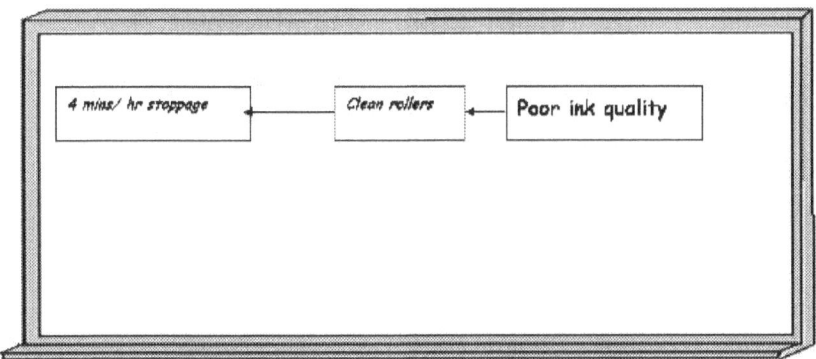

"What is it about the ink quality that causes you to clean the rollers?" asks Ralph.

Carl replies: "Well, the ink contains small particles which eventually build up on the surface of the roller".

"And why does the ink contain these particles? I would have imagined that a good quality ink would be particle-free".

Carl answers: "We buy one of the cheaper versions of ink."

Ralph adds two more boxes to his diagram on the whiteboard.

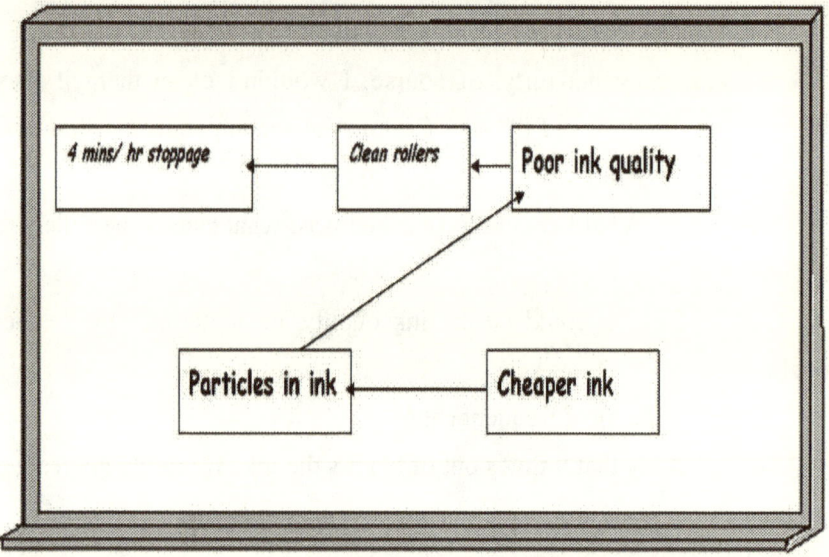

"Then if the root problem is that the ink is cheap, why don't we buy a more expensive version, which eliminates this problem completely?" asks Ralph.

"Because the Company won't pay any more money for ink! And the best particle-free quality ink costs about 50% more than we pay now."

"But you're just assuming that the Company won't pay more for ink, aren't you Carl? Let's look at this another way. Currently, you stop the machine for 4 minutes every hour, and let's say that on average the machine is only actually producing for 30 minutes each hour. So, this means that if you could eliminate this problem completely, you could increase your 30 minutes of production per hour, or let's say 5,000 balls per hour, to 34 minutes of production, or let's say 5,666 balls in that hour. Let me show you this on the whiteboard."

Ralph draws up the following table:

	Current	Proposed	
Production time per hour	30 min	34 min	+13%
Muda for ink problems	4 min	0 min	
Other Muda	26 min	26 min	
Production at 10,000 /hour	5,000	5,666	+13%

"So, if we spend 50% more on ink, then we can increase production by 13%. Are my figures correct, Carl?"

"Yes, I think so. But it's not worth spending 50% more on ink to get 13% more production, is it?"

"Are you so sure? I'm not the expert here, but I guess that the ink represents no more than 2% or 3 % of the total cost of a ball; do you have the exact figure, Andy?"

"Sure. A typical ball's costs are made up of 60% leather, 25% depreciation, 1% ink and 14% labour."

"Thanks Andy. Now, Carl, we are going to work out whether it is worth our while spending more on ink, or not. Let's put this into a table."

Making himself a fresh space on one of the whiteboards, Ralph writes out the following table:

Current cost of 100 balls		Proposed cost 113 balls	
Leather 60%.......	$6,000	+13%	6,780
Ink 1%...... ..	100	+13% +50%...	170
Labor 14%	1,400	unchanged........	1,400
Depreciation 25%....	2,500	unchanged........	1,400
Total	10,000	Total	10,850
Cost per ball	100	Cost per ball	96.0
			- 4%

"Do you see, Carl, and everyone, that spending a little more to reduce the Muda actually not only increases our productivity by 13% but also reduces our costs by 4%? Now you can see how important your role is, in all this. The information you provide on the Production Schedule document can help Andy and the supervisors to evaluate whether it is better to pay for an increase in quality of a raw material, or even whether it is worth purchasing a new machine or not. And you see where you benefit too, don't you? Surely your life will be a lot less stressful if you do not have to stop your machine every hour to clean it, just because the company you work for is so cheapskate that it wants to save a few cents on every liter of ink purchased?"

Carl replies, "Okay. It certainly sounds worthwhile enough to give this system a try."

Ralph says to Carl, "Thanks for being my guinea pig there, Carl." Then he addresses the group as a whole, "Does anyone else have any questions?"

So far, Jack the supervisor of the group, has said nothing. I notice that he is looking uncomfortable. But it appears that he is summoning up his courage to ask his question.

92

"Ralph, I am worried that all this attention on Muda and production volumes will cause our people to take their eyes off quality. You see, over the last two years we have got the percentage of internal rejects down from 5% to 3%, and my concern is that working with this new system will cause the internal reject percentage to go up again And, just in case you didn't know, all of us here are on a quality bonus scheme."

"Thank you, Jack, for raising a very important point," says Ralph. "Two points to consider. First of all, remember that producing a poor quality product is Muda, and so it should be monitored and quantified in this system. So, rather than diverting attention away from quality, it incorporates it totally. The second point is one of experience. In many instances where we've installed this type of system, the quality indicators actually improve by up to 50 %. However, to put you at ease, and to remove the fear of your pocket been affected (*patting his trouser leg as he says this*), I will give you a guarantee that your quality indicators will at the very least stay at the current three percent as a result of installing this."

The reference to Jack's pocket produces some laughter, and some comments along the lines of, "trust a Scotsman to look after our money!" But I can see that the operators and Jack have bought into trying out the system.

Ralph concludes: "To sum up, this is how the new system will work. The machinist is responsible for completing the 'Production Control Sheet' every hour in terms of produced quantities, and he also uses the document to detect and to assign all the causes of production losses.

The supervisor is responsible for providing the work plan in the document, and the calculations of the totals at the end of the shift.

More importantly though, the supervisor uses the document to decide every hour where he should take an action to generate the maximum impact in his area. For example, let's say that in an hourly tour, he sees that 3 of his machines have reported lost times of 5, 10 and 23 minutes respectively. He decides to focus on the machine with the largest variance. On this machine, there are 4 lost time causes that hour, of 3, 4, 5 and 11 minutes, which obviously add up to 23 in total. He then decides to tackle the problem causing the 11 minutes lost time, and thus eliminates the biggest problem during that hour in his area. The following hour, the area's performance should be better by those 11 minutes (unless, of course, something else occurs in the meantime!).

When he has finished the calculations of the totals at the end of his shift, the supervisor enters the data summarized in his 'Daily Production Report', and then uses the document as an analysis point in his ten-minute 'Daily Production Review Meeting' the following day with his Production Manager.

At the end of this meeting, the supervisor then sends the completed 'Production Control Sheet' document to whoever is responsible for maintaining and updating production planning standards and cost information. This person checks the actual against each standard, correcting if necessary, and informing the Planning Department of the changes. Are there any questions?" concludes Ralph.

Everyone seems to be clear on Ralph's presentation, because, to my surprise, there are no questions.

"Andy, are you and your team willing to give this system a shot?" asks Ralph, in front of everyone. Looking around, I sense a general murmur of approval.

"Yes, I believe we are. We'll need a few days to draw up the formats to adapt the concept to each specific area, and we'll probably maintain the existing system alongside for a while at least, until we see that the new documents do everything that the old system does. Then, when it is working, and everyone is used to it, we can look to computerize as much of the documents as possible, and then to eliminate the current Job Card system. But that's looking perhaps too far ahead, for the moment. We'll run this thing starting on Monday, everyone agreed?"

Everyone agrees. Monday is D-Day.

Chapter 7. Unleash the hidden power of your people

"If you do not do things you fear, fear controls your life."
Glenn Ford, actor.
"Do the thing you fear and the death of fear is certain."
Ralph Waldo Emerson, writer and philosopher.
"Courage is not the lack of fear or absence of fear; it is the mastery of fear."
Mark Twain, writer.

"Let's talk about now the second of the three steps you mentioned. What do you think you will achieve by carrying out these Performance Improvement Workshops, or Champions' Workshops as you're calling them, with the workers?" I ask of Ralph. "I mean, wouldn't it be better to train the supervisors or even some of the managers? I mean, what can you realistically expect to achieve from the workers? They have had no experience in productivity improvement; that's our job, as management and supervision. Or have I got it all wrong?"

"My God, you do try to pack a whole load of questions into one packet, don't you? I'll try to take you through the process step by step," responds Ralph. "The objective of the workshop is to produce outstanding results through helping the workers to recover their confidence and pride in their own abilities, and to become aware of some of the potential they have within. A secondary objective is to break down some of the barriers and cultural differences between the workers and the management team."

"And how do you intend to achieve these wonders?" I ask, perhaps with a tinge of scepticism.

"The way these objectives are achieved is to get the workers to a position where they realize their own power, and develop confidence in their abilities to deliver dramatic improvements to the company. This is done by setting them demanding objectives and helping them through the process step by step. At the outset of the workshop, we tell the workers that their goals for the next 3 days are to make their work:

faster;

with less cost;

with better quality;

safer;

more fun, and

all this without incurring extra costs for the company. We tell them that at the end of the 3 days they will present their improvement projects to senior management, and that they will cause a great impact because their projects will typically present productivity improvements of 20%, 30% or more in their specific areas. This normally provokes some disbelief."

"You can bet your socks it'll cause just that reaction here, buddy," I interrupt. "How the heck do you overcome that?"

"Several ways. We do some exercises then on making them aware of their perceptions, their beliefs, their fears, and how limiting they are on their lives. These I call their 'Chains', which by the way we all have to one degree or another. And we follow that with some other exercises demonstrating that dramatic improvements can be achieved through changing methods, systems and procedures at work. It is perhaps these real-life exercises which get the workers to understand and really take on board the concepts, like Muda, which seem at first academic and not related to the work they do, nor their personal situation outside of work. But after a while, they see that what they are learning is equally useful at home, as at work," explains Ralph.

He goes on: "But that's not all. And here's where you come in. The first thing I ask is that you get Bill Braces to open the Workshop, explaining his total support for this process and making clear his positive expectations. The second thing I need is this: in order to run a successful worker performance improvement Workshop, it is vitally important to remove the workers' fear of losing their jobs very early on. Asking a worker to contribute ideas of how to improve company performance when he feels that his job may be at risk is a bit like asking a turkey to vote for Christmas in England or for Thanksgiving in the USA. If a manager is serious about involving his people in the running of the business, but he uses some ideas proposed by the workers to reduce their number, he will find that the flow of positive ideas will dry up forever, and the level of trust and motivation in his workforce will be close to zero. That's why before starting the Workshop I request that you, Andy, get me a letter from Bill, the General Manager, in which he states that there will be no job losses as a result of the Workshop. If the topic comes up in the Workshop, I normally show this letter to the workers. Better still if Bill, when he opens the workshop personally with a short speech, 5 to 10 minutes maximum, can make the same commitment verbally."

I need some time to digest this.

"Ok, suppose for a moment that they are not afraid of losing their jobs, or causing their companions to lose theirs, there still is the problem that the workers themselves believe that they are not creative, that management is supposed to come up with the good ideas. I know many of the workers, and I suspect that they will feel overawed, that they will not be able to do this. I also know that this is the generalised belief of our management team."

Ralph nods his agreement. "And it's not only your management team, my friend. It is the generalized belief, or the dominant paradigm in the majority of industries. Look, I brought something to show you. I collect quotations by wise people from everywhere, and I think this one is quite relevant to what we are talking about."

With these words, he searches through the mountain of papers in his briefcase, and finally hands me a sheet with the satisfied grin of having found the treasure.

What I see and read is:

"We are going to win and you in the industrial West are going to lose. There is nothing you can do about it, because the reasons for your failure are within yourselves. For you, the essence of management is to take the ideas from the heads of management and place them in the hands of the workers."
Konoke Matushita, Japanese industrialist.

"How do you feel about what you have just read?" Ralph asks me.

"I have several reactions. In part, I feel angry at the arrogance of this guy. Also, I feel that there is some truth in what he saying, but it bothers me and I'm not sure why. I know that Japan has grown in an impressive way, from when it was in ruins after the Second World War, to today, occupying the position of the second economic power in the world, with only a mere fraction of the natural resources of the first power, the United States. And it has much less resources than many other countries. From what I have read and studied, I know that Japan does not owe its growth to its natural resources, but to its culture, which is a culture far more respectful than ours, and to its philosophy, which includes concepts like 'kaizen' or 'continuous improvement'."

"And when you think about kaizen, do you think that the improvement ideas all come from the managers, or do workers also contribute?" insists Ralph.

"Look, I know that they have achieved a great deal of collaboration between workers and managers, but that's a cultural thing. I mean, that sort of thing would not work here, singing the company hymn at the start of each day. They would throw us out through the door for being ridiculous. You can't turn our people into docile Japanese!"

"I totally agree with you. Transplanting the Japanese culture here would be a huge disaster. However, just consider this: do you think that your people have more creativity and initiative than their Japanese equivalents?"

I consider this for some seconds before replying. "Of course. Some of the solutions which our people have found to problems have been amazing. And the Japanese are famous for being very good at copying and implementing good ideas from elsewhere, but not so much for generating original ideas themselves."

"So then, why then is it difficult for you to accept that your people can generate ideas which contribute to the business, that their ideas can even be better than your managers' ideas?"

I sense that with this question Ralph is getting close to a sensitive part within me, which I have not wanted to face. I tell him: "you know what? I think that I have never really made myself the time to ask myself if our people can really contribute more than they are actually doing. And deep down, I must recognize that maybe it is because of a fear, the fear that I'm seen to be running the business badly and not as it should be."

To my great surprise, Ralph tells me: "I congratulate you for your openness and honesty. You have just hit bull's eye on the real reason why many managers do not dare to trust in the capacities of their people. Many, many managers deep down feel insecure about themselves. They feel, often unconsciously, that they have to be always proving that they are the best, the most intelligent and everything else, if not their people will not respect them. So, because of this belief that managers have to be those who have the best ideas, there is the fear of losing the respect of their subordinates, of their peers and their superiors, and the fear of their own failure. My interpretation of the words of Matushita, 'the reasons for their failure are within themselves', is that our fears are that which   prevent us from making the leap to trust in our people."

Fascinated, but still not convinced, I say to Ralph: "I never would have thought that fear is an important factor in the behavior of a manager. I can easily visualize it in the case of the worker, but not for a manager, to be frank. Can you give me some examples of behavior that you have observed which make you believe that managers act out of fear?"

"Andy, do you know what is the most frequent complaint that I hear from workers about their managers? They tell me that when the managers walk through their work areas, they do not even salute, they don't smile, they don't even say 'good morning'. Not every manager, agreed, but many, the majority. I have spoken with hundreds of managers about this and I am convinced that they do not do this consciously; they tell me that they think that the workers do not want managers to speak to them, that it would make them uncomfortable. But deep down, this is just an intellectual justification to cover up the fear, the fear that the workers would reject them."

I'm having trouble admitting it, but now, listening to Ralph and thinking about it, I see that when I used to visit other companies, often I would arrange it to avoid too much contact with the workers. I remember an embarrassing incident: when I was doing my general training in UniBall, I spent some time on one of the production lines accompanying a group of workers who worked there. They told me in no uncertain terms that the bosses didn't speak to them, and that they thought that I, just like all the others, would also forget them in the years to come. "Bosses don't respect us and they expect that we respect them, but things don't work that way, " they used to say to me. I told them that this would never happen to

102

me. But, one day some three years later, when I was Assistant Production Manager, I was showing the plant to a group of important visitors and we passed through that section which I had not visited in some time. I was so absorbed in showing the visitors how much I knew of the production lines that it didn't even occur to me to introduce the workers; if I remember correctly, I went directly there without saluting them. When we were going, I heard one worker say to another, "See? Just like all the others. Too much of a boss to even say a word to us!" My blood froze when I heard this, but I pretended not to hear and rushed my visitors along.

I confide this memory to Ralph. "Maybe you're right. Maybe I was afraid that the visitors would realize that I knew much less about that section than the workers. But my action was totally unconscious, not intentional or premeditated."

"That's how it is most of the time, Andy," Ralph consoles me. "We'll speak more about beliefs and unconscious behaviors shortly. But, can you see now how fears, whether conscious or unconscious, can affect behavior?" he asks me.

"I'm starting to see. But, to get back to our starting point, surely it's not enough to just remove the workers' fear of losing their jobs so that they propose creative solutions for the company?"

"Your point is valid. There is another fear behind this, the fear of failure. To combat the fear of failure, quite often I show videos of other workshops in which they can see that workers like themselves, but in other companies, have obtained similar results. Seeing the videos they realize that they are no different from their counterparts in other companies (often they think they are better!)".

"Seeing other workers do it is enough to get them to risk looking funny or stupid in front of their peers or management? And even if you can get them to take the risk of looking silly, how do you get them to be creative?" I persist.

"You could rephrase your first question as: are you prepared to let a few minutes of possible embarrassment stand in the way of your life-time personal growth? Or do you consider that not looking silly is more important than an opportunity to develop yourself professionally? Phrased that way, most people decide that if the price of long-term personal growth is a few moments of ridicule, then they will accept to pay that price. As regards the unspoken or unconscious belief that they as workers are not qualified or not able to suggest improvement ideas, this I tackle by asking them to do various exercises, one of which may be the nine dots exercise. Do you know it?" asks Ralph.

"I think I've seen it somewhere before, but I've forgotten it. Please remind me," I request.

Ralph draws out 9 circles on the whiteboard, as shown below:

O   O   O

O   O   O

O   O   O

"Just join the nine dots together with only four continuous and straight lines. Continuous means that you cannot lift your pen off the paper. If you draw a line going back on itself, something like this, it counts as 3 lines, not two:

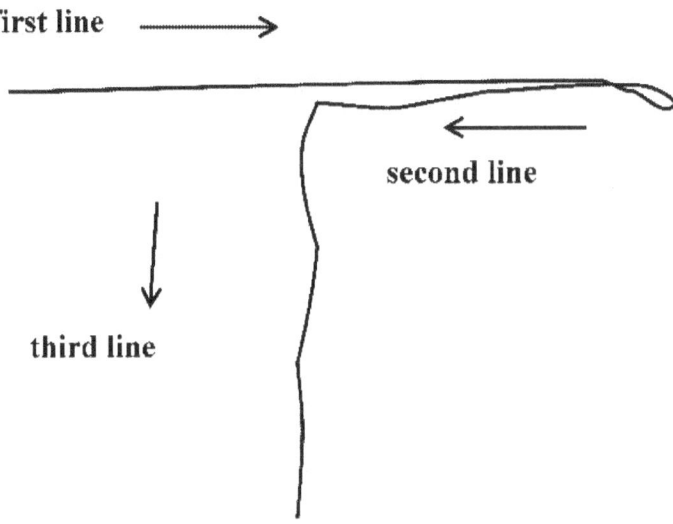

first line

second line

third line

If you do not remember the exercise, please take a few minutes now to do it."

I spend a few minutes doodling on my notepad, and eventually say to Ralph, "Ok, that's enough, I've forgotten, show me the solution, please."

Ralph obliges, saying: "Normally only one person in a workshop of 20 will guess the answer (excluding those who know the answer already). Often some people know that they've seen the exercise before, but have forgotten the solution and more importantly have forgotten, or not been told, the message associated with it. The reason why most people fail to see the solution is because they think (or believe) that it is necessary to stay within the confines of the nine dots, as if there were an imaginary box surrounding them. The solution consists in going outside the imaginary boundaries. Notice that these boundaries do not exist in the instruction to the exercise. The only place where the boundaries exist is in the mind of the person doing the exercise, and so it is what a person believes that limits him or her even though there is no basis for that belief."

Ralph moves again towards my whiteboard to draw the solution.

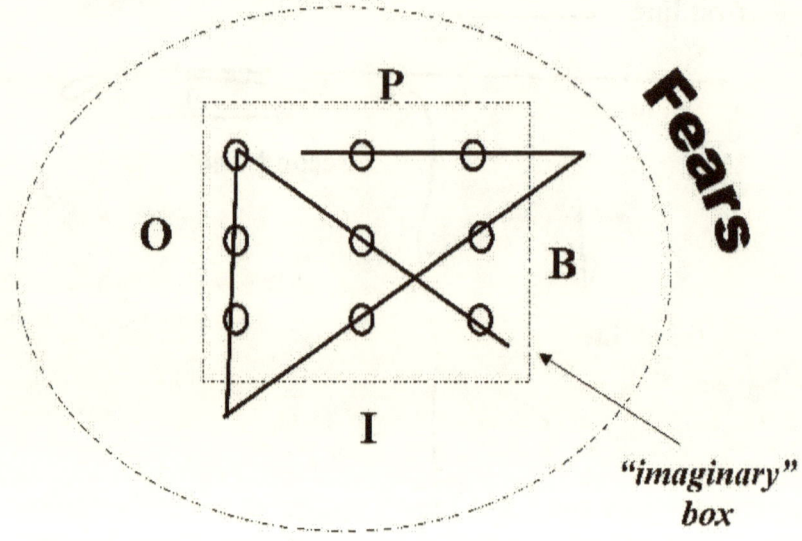

"*imaginary*"
box

When he finishes his drawing, Ralph explains it:

"Why should you hold yourself back from experiencing your full potential because of some rules which you have invented for yourself but which in reality don't exist? No one said that you couldn't go outside the box. Only your imagination told you so. But our imagination is so powerful, that it can hold us back, just as if it were a chain hanging around our necks."

"That's a powerful analogy, there. What do the letters *P, B, I* and *O* stand for?" I ask.

"Once they have seen the answer, I tell the worker participants that this imaginary box is called the 'box of mediocrity'. And the four walls of the box have names as well, easy to remember using the acronym 'PIBO'. **P** stands for **perceptions**, the **I** stands for **interpretations**, **B** stands for **beliefs** and the **O** stands for **opinions**. So our perceptions, interpretations, beliefs and opinions can hold us back just as if they were real concrete walls around us. If we believe that we can't do something, even if that belief is totally untrue, the end result is that we won't be able to do that thing.

106

And around these 4 walls, there is an even thicker wall called 'Fears'. In fact, these imaginary walls are so dangerous, precisely because we are not even aware that they are there, and are holding us back. Often we humans are only too ready to fight to defend our beliefs, opinions, perceptions or interpretations as if they were an integral part of our personality. Sad as it is, these walls are so powerful in our minds that human beings are the only animals which will kill those of their own kind because they do not share the same beliefs. Catholics or Protestants, Christians or atheists, Arabs or Jews, capitalist or communist, football supporters of United or Rangers, black or white, are only some of the ways we human beings have found to separate us into groups and thus justify the killing of those in the other groups. The question to ask about a belief or fear is: is this particular belief or fear inhibiting me from achieving my potential, or is it helping me? The workers come to the conclusion that the belief that they are not capable of generating improvements limits their growth and opportunities; so I then invite them to replace this negative belief with another more positive and powerful one, such as:

'I can generate spectacular ideas', or

'I am the expert in my area', or

'Management respects and values my opinions', and so on."

"Are there any other dangerous or limiting beliefs you have to contend with in these workshops?" I feel the need to enquire.

"There is still another harmful belief which acts as a powerful chain and which needs to be broken," begins Ralph. "This is the belief that we are already working the best we can in the best possible way. To demonstrate that this is not so, I provide the workers with a new understanding. This is the Japanese concept of Muda, which I've already covered with you and the supervisors. The workers can easily grasp intellectually the concept of Muda. But they must get an understanding of it in their hearts, before they really will believe themselves capable of generating terrific improvements. The human brain is a magnificent tool, but our real strength comes from our passion and our beliefs, which are held in the heart, and this is where our deepest understandings lie. So, to transfer the concept of Muda from brain understanding to heart understanding, we look at a video of a case study, where dramatic improvements have been achieved before: for example, reduction of delivery time by 90 % and a 300 % increase in productivity. Then we play a simulation game, which by the way is fun to do, in which the teams are given the task of constructing a product (or a budget in the case of an administration or service group). At the end of this exercise, the teams come to realize through direct experience that they were operating at the level of 90 % Muda and were totally unaware of it. They learn to distinguish from activity and productivity in the best way--- through their own direct experience. We also get them to do various other exercises to get them to understand the concept through living it. This puts in practice the Chinese proverb:

> 'Tell me and I may understand,
> Show me and I may remember,
> Involve me and I will be committed'."

"Why do they have these negative beliefs about themselves, Ralph? I mean, this is usual, isn't it, it is not just this company?"

"Yes, it is very usual, and it is not just the workers with disempowering belief systems; it's all of us. We all of us operate well below our potential, and in the main it is because of how we've been brought up, educated, and conditioned by society. I like to refer to all these conditionings as our ´chains´."

"Several times you have used that word, 'chains'. Any special reason for that?" Curious as I always am.

"You are asking me to explain the whole psychology of the Champions' Workshop, and that is quite a long answer. It's like asking your driving instructor how your car engine works, when your most urgent need is to learn how to drive the car, and for that it is not absolutely necessary to know how the engine works. Are you willing to dedicate some time to this, Andy?"

"Let me explain something about myself, Ralph. Even though I studied Engineering in University, my true passion has always been people. I almost decided to study psychology. But when I graduated, I looked for a job in management, instead of engineering, precisely because of that interest. So, of course I want to invest the time necessary in order to learn how to help my people to develop!"

"Great! At your service! To start off, I believe that there are 3 factors which prevent people from reaching their true potential: fear, limiting beliefs, and outdated systems and procedures. All of these factors I call 'Chains', after understanding the behaviour of circus elephants. Surely you've seen them. These powerful animals seem to be controlled by a simple rope or belt tying their leg to a small stake in the ground."

"Do you know how the trainer manages to get the elephant to behave this way, Andy?" Ralph asks me.

I have to admit that I've seen circus elephants many times, but I have no idea how the trainers tame them. But Ralph is undoubtedly going to explain it all to me.

"How the elephant trainer achieves this provides some revealing insights on human behaviour. What happens is this: soon after the elephant is born, the trainer takes the baby elephant and attaches a thick, strong chain to one of its hind legs, attaching the other end of the chain to a wide and strong column. The baby pulls at the chain, screaming and crying, but to no avail, as the chain is too strong for him. He grows tired, frustrated, saddened and dispirited; the chain cuts into his leg and hurts him, so after a while he starts to pull on the chain with less force than before.

When, sometime later, the trainer changes the chain for a thinner, weaker one, the elephant doesn't notice, because by then he is pulling with less enthusiasm and belief than in the beginning. He's doesn't pull now with the same strength. Over time, the trainer gradually reduces the chain thickness, and all the while the elephant pulls with less and less force, perhaps from time to time twitching his leg out of irritation or reflex. Comes the day when our elephant friend stops pulling whenever he *FEELS* something attached to his leg. He's been conditioned to think that when he feels that there is something attached to his leg, it's painful and useless to try to pull himself free, and so he doesn't even try. And so a 5 tonne elephant with enormous strength eventually is brought to immobility by a slender cord that he could break without a drop of sweat. Notice that he has the power, but he doesn't use it, because he THINKS he can't. The reality is that he has many times the power required, and it is only the THOUGHT or mistaken belief that he can't which is enough to render him powerless."

"Fascinating. I didn't know that. So, whenever we do not see the solution to the 9 dots, you are saying that it's because we are wearing our chains?" I ask Ralph.

"Precisely, because the only thing which stops us from seeing the solution is the mistaken (and often unconscious) belief that we cannot go outside of the box, just like the elephant that thinks that he cannot move. In both cases the reality is different, but that doesn't matter; our mental chains are stronger than any real chain. Just like the circus elephants, we human beings also have our own 'chains'. Most of us operate well beneath our capabilities and potential, and just like the elephant, we don't even begin to suspect that we're only using a fraction of our power. But there is a slight difference: the elephant does have at least a thin rope, which physically represents the chain, and so something of his beliefs is based on a physical reality. But in the case of human beings, our chains are usually imaginary, that is they only exist in our heads. So, we humans limit ourselves in an unconscious way, just as the elephant does, or more so. A singer-songwriter called Howard Jones had a hit some years back with a song called, 'Mental Chains'. Do you remember the verse? It went something like: 'don't crack up, bend your mind, see both sides, throw off your mental chains, whoa, whoa, whoa'."

I can't help smiling at Ralph's unmelodious and unexpected singing. But, so as not to embarrass him, I continued: "Ralph, that is all powerful stuff! Tell me, where do you think our mental chains come from?"

"That is a question which is keeping busy an army of psychologists these days. But, as I pointed out before, I think that many of them are our own hidden fears. They come from the little blows that life deals out to us all continuously and which slowly and accumulatively condition our subconscious. We may receive life's blows within our families or within our schools, and though each blow may be tiny, as we pick them up one by one, the cumulative effect is as limiting as the elephant's chain. In school and at home, we are conditioned to believe that: 'you can't do that!', or 'you'll never be good enough to do that!', or 'stop day-dreaming and get real!'. Studies have shown that by the time a child is 8 years old, he or she has heard the word 'NO' 100,000 times! Albert Einstein thought that human beings only use 5% to 10% of their brain! In other words, we all have the potential to be geniuses, but only a few of us *even dare* to use a greater part of our potential. Why? Because if we do something which makes us stand out from the vast majority of other human beings, we think that we'll be classified as weird, and we would be socially excluded. And as we are primarily social creatures, in general we would do anything to be part of the group, even paying the cost of dimming our talents. We've all heard stories of these brilliant kids who act wildly and perform well below their capabilities. Why is that? Because it is more important for them at that age to be in the 'in crowd' than to stand out or to be different from the normal."

"So, because we fear being socially ostracised, we settle for mediocrity?"

"Right, Andy. You've got a gift for summing up in a few words. My belief is that the first chains that we human beings accept on ourselves are the many different faces of fear: fear of being different, fear of being wrong, fear of looking foolish, fear of failure, fear of criticism, fear of our bosses, fear of loneliness, and so on. Whether you are consciously aware of it or not, fear is the dominant force in many of our companies and institutions today, be they manufacturing, services or state-owned, and it is the biggest obstacle against achieving dramatic productivity improvements. Many employees are simply afraid to speak out, to push for improvements, to fight for what they believe is right. 'No-one listens here, so what's the point? I just do what they pay me to do.' 'Once I said what I thought, and since then they have me pegged as a troublemaker. It's just not worth it!' Behind statements like these, there is the hidden fear of losing their jobs because of speaking up, or of being punished, or of being cold-shouldered, etcetera."

"I can see how that fear is everywhere, now that you point it out to me. I guess that I had never really thought about it before. But why is fear so prevalent? I mean, I don't think that it starts in our companies, or have I got it all wrong?" I interrogate.

"Andy, I would like to point out that I am just explaining my beliefs to you. I do not claim to be the owner of the absolute truth. Therefore, let's talk about my beliefs if you wish, but please keep in mind that the very second that someone can show me how my beliefs are not empowering, but limiting, I will seek out a more powerful set of beliefs. At least I am trying to keep an open mind, to be aware of how my beliefs may limit me or may empower me, so I want you to question everything, and not to accept any external belief until you have totally evaluated it for yourself. Agreed?"

"Take it as a done thing, buddy!" I like his frank and open style of conversation with me. "But I'm not going to let you off the hook so easily; you haven't answered my question. Why do you think fears are so prevalent?"

"Right, then. I believe that fear is so common because it is the way in which our education system, our religious organizations, our societies and cultures have historically controlled us. For example, when we're kids at home, adults say to us: 'if you don't eat up your vegetables, you won't grow up big and strong', or 'if you don't behave, Santa Claus won't bring you any Christmas presents'. In fact, the well-known Christmas song 'Santa Claus is coming to town' says as much. Remember the verse?"

And before I could stop him, Ralph was off singing again. I look hastily to make sure the office door is shut, and hope that no-one outside can hear what is going on.

" 'He's making his list, he's checking it twice, he's going to find out who's naughty and nice, Santa Claus is coming to town.' The song implicitly threatens the child with no Christmas presents if he or she behaves badly. This is an example of control through the fear of loss in the home.

At school, our teachers say to us, 'if you fail your tests, we are going to make you stand in the corner wearing a dunce's cap', or 'if you don't do your homework, you'll end up cleaning floors and toilets', or 'if you don't go to University, you'll end up in a dead-end job'.

Our organized religions tell us, 'if you don't go to church on Sundays, you're committing a sin,' and, 'if you commit sins, when you die, you'll go to hell', or 'if you do not treat your brothers well, your negative karma will follow you in your next life'.

Even in the workplace, the unwritten rule is: 'if you don't do unquestioningly what your boss says, you will lose your job'.

Depending on the culture or society in which we live, our behaviour is controlled by social or cultural 'taboos'. For example, 'tell lies and your nose will grow longer', or 'behave badly and you'll turn into a donkey'.

Underneath all of these sayings is the idea of punishment: 'if you don't do such and such a thing, something bad will happen to you'. So you can see that, in school, at home, at work or in society in general, fear is the tool most often used to control our behaviours and to make us fit in.

The problem is that fear is a very effective brake against us exercising our natural creativity. 'Better not do anything different because people will only laugh at me'. So as a consequence, we have millions of people acting out their lives using only a fraction of their potential, living lives as someone once expressed, 'in quiet desperation'."

"Ralph, you've just criticized about everybody going for all the evils in society. Tell me. Do you have *any* friends? Because you're going to need them with the amount of enemies you can make for yourself, speaking like that! But seriously, there are many people who would hate you, or even kill you, if they heard you speaking like that!"

"Yes, Andy, I'm aware of that. However, I want to stress that I am not criticizing our family lives, our schools, religions or societies: I am merely commenting on what is, on what I see, and on what is my belief. I believe that our parents and teachers and others have educated us in the best and only way they knew: by repeating the behaviours that they experienced and observed around themselves as they were growing up. Therefore, I am not blaming anyone. I know that I have made many mistakes with my children and in my own relationships. I am not judging, only observing."

"If it's not too personal a question, Ralph, do you mind giving me an example of a mistake you made?" I ask this question because I'm still grappling to see the practical effect of these 'fears' and 'chains' in the real world of business.

Ralph ponders a few moments, then replies: "Sure. It is an embarrassing and painful memory, but here goes. Some ten years back, I was a Country Head in the consultancy where I was working at the time, and I had some 30 consultants reporting to me. We had regular monthly Company meetings, as I recall, because with consultants working at different locations all over the country, it was necessary to get everybody together from time to time in order to maintain some sort of team spirit and effective communications. Well, towards the end of one of these meetings, I asked were there any questions. A junior consultant, called Eva, raised her hand. Her question was a personal one, not related to the business items we had been discussing. My first thought, upon hearing her question, was: 'what a stupid question!'. If I had just restricted myself to the thought, there would have been no problem. But that is not what happened. You've heard the saying: 'engage brain, before opening mouth'? Well, I must admit, my mouth was working on automatic pilot. I unthinkingly said out loud that I thought it was a stupid question. A silence fell across the meeting room. I asked were there any further questions, and there being none, I concluded the meeting, and thought no more of it.

During the next 6 months or so, I was vaguely aware that there were relatively few questions asked at the regular meetings, and these were normally asked by some of the managers. I assumed that this was because of the clarity of our presentations, and that everyone totally understood where the Company was going and why.

It was only when one of the consultants was promoted to Manager that I learnt the truth. The newly-promoted Manager confided to me that the consultants were afraid of asking me a question in meetings, because 'he would bite your head off, as he did to Eva'. I was dumbstruck. I mean, here was a group of highly educated people, all with MBA's and degrees, and presumably highly career-motivated, and they were afraid of asking me a question! Realizing how I had caused this situation, I set about to improve. It took me many months to recover the trust of some of the consultants, but I never recovered Eva's trust, and she left shortly afterwards. When I was transferred to this country, I resolved not to make that same mistake. For that reason, one of the most important rules that I apply in all the work I do, and in my personal life, is the following, which I'm going to leave with you as a gift."

Ralph pulls out from his briefcase a plaque, which says:

The only stupid question is the question you don't ask!

"Thank you, Ralph. What a great message," I say. "I guess it's true that all of us, at some time or other, have been in a large meeting and have not asked a question because we've thought that the meeting leader, or the other participants, would think we were stupid. I know I have refrained from asking questions, but usually it's an automatic or unconscious thing."

Ralph nods agreement, and goes to the whiteboard. "That's exactly what happens. It is as if there is a tiny weigh-scale inside our heads. On one side, there is the weight of the desire to improve oneself, which is always there, and I can improve myself by asking a question when I am unsure about something."

Ralph draws:

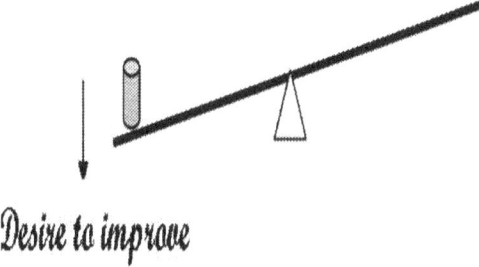

Desire to improve

"But then, unconsciously, on the other side of the scale, the fear of looking stupid places itself, and before we realize it, we are not asking the question."

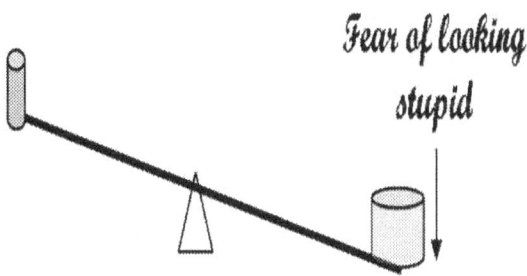

Fear of looking stupid

"And we cannot do anything about it, as long as this process is unconscious. The only way to overcome this fear of looking stupid is to make a **CONSCIOUS** decision, such as: 'I value my self-improvement and self-growth so much that the price I am prepared to pay is much, much greater than the fear of looking stupid'."

Ralph draws:

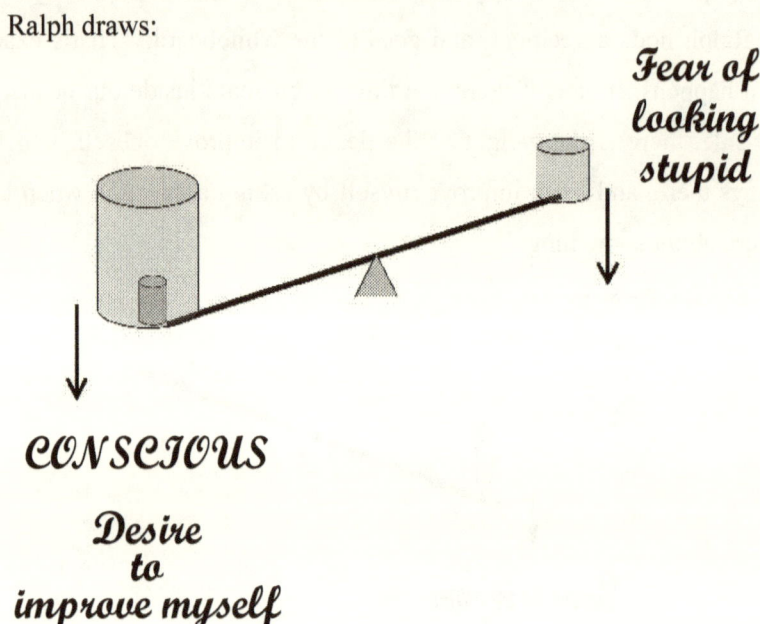

Fear of looking stupid

CONSCIOUS

Desire to improve myself

" 'Even if other people are still laughing at me 6 months afterwards, as long as I have learnt something useful and powerful for my personal growth, it is a price I am very happy to pay.' This is an example of an empowering belief, and is the invitation I extend to the workers in the Champions' Workshops, which they usually accept."

"Thank you again, Ralph, for sharing your own experience with me. I can see now why you feel so strongly about eliminating fears from the workplace. Let's have a natural break now, what do you think?"

"Good idea, Andy, I need to powder my nose too!"

Chapter 8. The Love-Based Culture

When, some 15 minutes later, we resume our meeting in my office, we spend some minutes talking about our families and about the latest turmoil in the currency markets. Eventually, I say, "Well, this is all interesting, but it is Muda, right?"

Ralph agrees. So I suggest that we continue with our topic of 'fears' and 'chains' in the company.

"Ralph, as you have thought so much about these things, what do you think we should do?"

"Look, I think it is time to break this vicious circle. It is time to replace fear as the main tool for control by love. That is the task before parents and teachers today: catch them while they are young, and educate without using fear as the primary tool. But what about the millions of adult people walking around on the face of the Earth today, held back by their fears? Is it too late for them? No, I don't think so. I think that there is a way out of this cultural trap. The way out of the trap is to break through the fear, and that is the purpose of this project which we're working on: to help to unleash people power as a route towards improving the Company's result. I think it is time to replace fear-based cultures with cultures based on love."

"What does a fear-based culture look like in a Company?" I feel that what Ralph is saying is very interesting, but I always have to be looking how to apply the theory to the practice, which is why I interrupt him with my questions. So far, I cannot see the practical application.

"The Fear-Based Culture (let's say FBC, for short) is where the boss applies fear (fear of losing the job, of withholding bonuses, salary increases or promotions) in order to get the results that he wants. And in the short run, it works. But in the longer term, the Fear-Based Culture

(FBC) actually harms the Company. .Employees are not motivated to improve things through using their own initiative; staff turnover is high; internal politics are rife; people spend a great deal of time either trying to curry favour with their bosses or to discredit their rivals; people are not willing to accept responsibility and are constantly trying to pass the buck, and to cover their asses by sending out reams of memos. The 'rat race' is a term coined for the FBC. And all of this has got to do with what started our conversation: the Champions' Workshop, which is designed to liberate peoples' creativity. Because the FBC also stifles the natural creativity of the company's employees for another reason: bosses are often afraid of not looking good, or of having their subordinates look better than themselves. So, when a subordinate comes up with a great idea to improve productivity in his area, the boss or supervisor may react in one of the following ways:

- discrediting or attacking the credibility or qualifications of the person who proposed the idea ('how can it be a good idea if *he* thought of it?');
- presenting the idea himself to upper management and taking the credit for it; or
- implementing the idea to improve productivity by reducing the number of people in the area.

Using one of these three strategies, the supervisor may gain a short-term payoff, but in the long run, he loses, the Company loses, and his subordinates lose, because the flow of great ideas will dry up forever as long as the FBC exists. Because of the FBC and because of the way we've been educated, many supervisors are not willing to recognize or accept that their people are the real experts in their business. A typical paradigm of a supervisor may be: 'the workers are not smart or intelligent enough to generate good ideas, that's why I'm here'. Consequently, believing that his people cannot contribute to the business more than the movements of their hands, arms or legs, the supervisor does not encourage them to do so. By the same token, many workers also believe that they are not good enough or educated enough to help the business in any different way."

"I guess that breaking the FBC within a Company would be a difficult or impossible job, right?"

"Difficult, but not impossible. At least, that is my belief!" replies Ralph. "I know it's not the generalized belief today, but the results we obtain in companies today is a function of the set of beliefs with which we manage those companies. And a different belief can bring about different and impressive results: that the workers can contribute enormously to a Company's success once their chains are broken. Because they work day in day out, directly with the products, machines, processes and clients, they know through their own direct experience what really goes on, much more so than anybody else in the company. Maybe they cannot express themselves as fluently as some University-educated supervisor, but that does not mean that they are not intelligent. Their intelligence is different, it is more intuitive than academic. The worker is often able to produce an excellent result, but he cannot easily explain how he does it, he simply just does it. To give an example: Diego Maradona, the famous Argentine soccer player, who was for a time rated the best player in the world, can produce wizardry with the ball. But ask him to explain how he does it and he cannot. On a purely verbal scale, a supervisor would probably judge him as being uneducated (and unfortunately too often, many supervisors and managers equate uneducated with being stupid). With a ball, Maradona displays a practical genius. Imagine the loss to the company if a supervisor or manager lets a Maradona go, just because the way he speaks shows that he came from the poor part of town!"

"You know what, Ralph? I'm thinking about a book I read a while ago by Edward de Bono, the guy who 'invented' lateral thinking and many other thinking styles. He says that there are about 16 different types of intelligence. Some are, for example: oratorical or verbal; numerical or mathematical; bodily co-ordination; musical; spatial or the ability to think in 3 dimensions; imaginative; intuitive; interpersonal or people intelligence, the so-called 'emotional intelligence', and entrepreneurial, and others which I can't remember right now. But the point I'm getting at is that the traditional school systems focus mainly on the basics, the 3 Rs: reading, writing and arithmetic, almost ignoring the other intelligence types (at least it was so when my generation was growing up, although I believe that many modern schools are attempting to be more broad in their coverage). So, a Diego Maradona-type kid, gifted with a high degree of co-ordination and spatial intelligences, would nevertheless be considered below average by a 'normal' system school."

"Good point. Did you know that Albert Einstein apparently didn't speak until he was nearly 5 years old? If that is so, how would a normal school today evaluate the greatest genius of the last century? Would we stifle his genius?"

"Probably so. And it is true that his greatest intelligence was a fantastic imagination. He thought up the Theory of relativity by imagining what it must be like to travel alongside a beam of light. But, it is also said that he couldn't remember his own telephone number! Thinking about that, it occurs to me that telephone numbers are normally more or less randomly distributed in packets of 7 or 8 digits, and that's a bit like how our natural intelligences are: randomly distributed with some numbers repeated, and others omitted. We all have intuitive and imaginative intelligences to some degree, but many people work in jobs where these types of intelligences are totally under-utilized." I realize that this is the longest I have spoken for quite a while. I had left Ralph dominate the conversation. Time to redress the balance a little, I think, so I go on:

"How many companies are directly aware of the different types of intelligences of their employees, and how many actively try to find ways to unleash these intelligences for the benefit of the individual and the company? Because of a generalized Fear-Based Culture, I would guess 'very few'. This culture, which I'm sure exists in the vast majority of companies, has the effect of consolidating the executives' positions and their opportunities for advancement, rather than actively seeking the personal growth of each individual. What do you think, Ralph?"

Ralph goes to his briefcase, which seems to be on the verge of exploding with all the papers inside it, and pulls out a book. He rummages between its pages and points out a paragraph, which he asks me to read. The book is called 'Principle-Centered Leadership', by someone called Dr. Steven R. Covey. What I read is:

> *When I ask in my seminars, "How many of you would agree that the vast majority of the work force possess far more capability, creativity, talent, initiative, and resourcefulness than their present jobs allow or require them to use?" the affirmative response is about 99 %. In other words, we all admit that our greatest resources are being wasted and that poor human resource management hurts our bottom lines.*

"Interesting book, Ralph. May I borrow it?"

"I would prefer to lend you the first book of that same author, which is called, 'The 7 Habits of Highly Effective People'. It would make more sense to you, as 'Principle-Centered Leadership' draws heavily on it. I'll bring it in tomorrow. In fact, in that book, Dr Covey gives a very good explanation of what a paradigm is, and how it feels to experience a paradigm shift."

"And what do you think is the paradigm of the Fear-Based Culture?"

"Good question! Let me think. It seems to me that behind the FBC there is a paradigm about how business should be carried out. The underlying paradigm of the FBC could be 'survival of the fittest': each person for himself. People avoid taking initiative, and waste enormous amounts of time justifying their actions in needless memos. 'Ass-covering', I call it. The fear of failure is rife. And the fear of loneliness is also present. In order to avoid being alone, people tend to form groups: managers with managers, and workers with workers. The fear of loneliness also manifests itself as 'fear of them', with each group looking out for its own interests."

"So, when everyone talks about the importance of motivation, how does motivation work in a FBC?" I ask.

Ralph replies: "The main motivational model used in the FBC seems to be 'the carrot and the stick': the 'carrot' is obviously money as a reward for performance, and the 'stick' is dismissal or the fear of getting fired. This model has 2 defects as a model of the motivational psychology of a human being: it assumes that people are only interested in money, and that they are as easily motivated as the proverbial donkey. If we choose a management system based on the motivational psychology of donkeys, then we shouldn't be surprised if we get a donkey-type performance and culture. Individual aspirations, team effort, group pride, all of these are ignored. Time and studies have shown that most people do not produce consistent and outstanding performance under this system."

"Look, Ralph, I suppose that the obvious opposite to a Fear-Based Culture would be a Love-Based Culture. What would be the paradigm of a culture like that, and how would that culture be?"

"Once again, all I'm going to tell you are my beliefs. The Love-Based Culture (or let's say LBC for short) would have its own paradigm. This paradigm could be expressed as:"

Once more, Ralph goes to his briefcase of magic tricks, looks for a sheet of paper and hands it to me when he finds it. It says:

> *It is the primary responsibility of a manager or supervisor to develop and grow the talents and abilities of those people under his charge. As the individuals grow, so will the organization in which they work, and hence its profits.*

"You know something, Ralph. I don't much like that name: Love-Based Culture. Are you sure that our people won't think that this project is about setting up Company bedrooms for lunchtime quickies?" I ask, kidding.

Ralph appears unamused by my joke and replies: "The challenge is to replace the F. B. C. by the L. B. C., which is the Love-Based Culture. Perhaps it would be appropriate here to explain what I mean by Love-Based Culture. I will start off by covering what I don't mean. A LBC company is not some sort of hippy commune where everyone goes around smoking dope, having sex like rabbits and wearing 'make love, not war' T-shirts. Nor do I mean a soft culture where I allow you to do exactly what you want when you want, regardless of the best interests of the company. Nor do I mean a company where we start each shift with a Bible reading. A LBC is one where some basic human principles are applied:

act towards others as you would like them to act towards you if the situations were reversed;

respect the opinions of everyone regardless of their positions within the organization;

recognize everyone has something to teach you regardless of your position or theirs;

provide opportunities for growth and self-actualization of your employees;

provide an environment where your employees can enjoy being at work;

provide a bonus or profit sharing arrangement where employees can share in the benefits of the success of the company.

There is an excellent book out, which talks about how the practise of 'love' within companies could be. It is called, 'The Servant' by James C. Hunter, and its main theme is leadership styles. Hunter explains that in our 'Hollywood' culture, we use the word 'love' incorrectly. He says that much of the Bible was written in Greek, and in that language there are 4 words which express 4 different types of love, which we translate into only one word. For us, love is an emotion, but in the strict sense of the term, 'love' implies a verb, an action. To show love towards someone within the context of leadership in a company means *to identify and satisfy the legitimate needs of the employees and to remove all obstacles to their serving the clients.* And he emphasises that satisfying the employee's legitimate needs does not mean satisfying necessarily his *desires or wants*. Desires are not needs. If all your employees desire or want salaries to be tripled, and if you as their leader implement this, then you will bankrupt the company, and through this action you will not be satisfying their legitimate needs, which include stability and secure employment over the long term.

"That might sound like the bleating of an evangelist with his head in the clouds. How can you sell this philosophy to the pragmatic people in the world of business? In my gut, I'm thinking, how can you show me the practical application of what are undoubtedly spiritual values? Because spirituality and business do not mix, at least that is my belief!" To be frank, I feel somewhat uneasy about where this conversation is going.

Ralph jumps in, apparently unaware of my unease. "Look, if someone wants to think that I am a preacher, then fair enough, if that's his opinion! However, I feel that that there is nothing more practical than this philosophy. We live in an epoch in which the rate of change is faster that ever it was and what's more..........it's speeding up! Here are some interesting statistics for you," says Ralph, handing me a sheet that he pulls out from his briefcase, like a magician pulling a rabbit out of the hat at just the right moment:

RATE OF CHANGE STATISTICS

In 1900, the quantity of information available to the human race was duplicating at a rate of every 1500 years.

In 1969, the quantity of information available to the human race was duplicating at a rate of every 50 years.

In 1999, the quantity of information available to the human race was duplicating at a rate of every 5 years.

In 2005, the quantity of information available to the human race will duplicate at a rate of every 39 days!

Ralph continues: "We can express this phenomenon of the explosive growth in information in another way. In the 16th Century, when our societies were largely agricultural, a typical person in his lifetime would manage less information than appears in a typical day on a newspaper like the 'New York Times'! What does this mean to you, Andy?"

I take a few seconds to ponder this. "What it probably means is that, despite all the many gifted and talented managers and Directors that are currently around these days, it is probably true to say that there is no one who is capable of absorbing the increase in specialist knowledge in their fields at the rates we are currently seeing."

"You won't be surprised to learn that I agree with you, Andy. In my humble opinion, the only route, and I am indeed convinced that it is the ONLY ROUTE available for those companies which seriously intend to survive and prosper into the 21st Century is to involve EVERYBODY in their organization in this task of continually improving their businesses. As Jack Welch, the former CEO of General Electric once said: '**If the rate**

of change outside your organization is faster than the rate of change within your organization, then the end is in sight.'"

A sudden insight strikes me, like a little bulb turning itself on somewhere inside my head. "You know, Ralph, economists talk about a country's wealth in terms of Gross Domestic Product, and put a value on the assets in the country to arrive at the GDP figure. Then they talk about comparative productivities between countries in terms of GDP per head. However, the real assets of the country are its people, their level of education, their level of creativity and their motivation. All of these things are what really drives a country, yet they are not taken into account by any economic measurement I've ever heard of. I mean, look at the Japanese economy: in terms of natural mineral wealth, Japan must be one of the poorest countries on the face of the Earth. Yet after the destruction of the Second World War, *their government and industries invested enormous amounts in the education and training of their people*, and today Japan is the second economic powerhouse of the world, with a mere fraction of the natural advantages of mineral resources of the first economic power."

"You've hit on a good example. The Japanese investment in people has paid off handsomely giving evidence to the ancient Chinese proverb:

If you want one year of wealth; .... grow grain.

If you want 10 years of wealth; .... grow trees.

If you want one hundred years of wealth; .... grow people.

The key point, I believe, is that the responsibility for growing people is not just for the government alone. Companies also have a leading and powerful role to play. I believe that if education is solely a responsibility of the state, the economic system of that country will eventually fail. A question for you. You attended University: how much of what you learned at University do you actually use today in the work you do?" Ralph asks me.

"Probably 10% tops." I say.

"Right. With the exception of those people who studied very technical disciplines and continue to work in those fields, the majority of people answer in the region of 0 to 10 %. They say at the same time that their most valuable learning has actually been on the job," declares Ralph, warming up to his theme now. I could see that I have really hit on a hot button of his.

Ralph continues: "Let's express the same point in a more dramatic way. If a supervisor or manager, recognizing that his people only use a fraction of their abilities in their jobs, is not determined to help his people uncover and release more of their hidden talents, he is not only depriving that person of growth opportunities, he is also depriving his company of the full benefit of that person's talents, and furthermore he will deny his country the full contribution of one of its most valuable resources towards improving the economy and the well-being of all."

"But how do we really know that people are only using a tiny fraction of their talents? Even if I accept what you told me about Albert Einstein saying that we use only 10% of our brains, and that Dr. Steven Covey reckons that people have far more abilities than they use in their work, it still all seems a bit theoretical to me, I'm having difficulty seeing it in practice."

"A little while ago, you said that it sounds like the preaching of an evangelist and that you find it difficult to see the practical application of spiritual values, correct? Well, we are here because we want to increase productivity, right, and if we consider that our most valuable resources are our people, then don't you think that we should consider the totality of a human being within our productivity equation?"

"Wait a minute, Ralph. You've lost me. What do you mean by the totality of a human being?"

"We say that a human being is made up of 3 parts: the body, the mind, and the heart or spirit or passion. For me, the terms heart, spirit and passion are interchangeable. Without thinking about any religion here, I think that we would all agree that a human being is much more than just his body, right?"

"Of course," I say.

""We all can agree that human beings also bring into the game of life something which we call a brain. Are you okay with that?"

"Sure, " I affirm.

"Now, when you consider the greatest sporting achievements, often we can see that a team with less talent or skill can win the trophy because of its fighting spirit, because of its passion, because of its heart, because of its commitment. Does that ring familiar?"

"Yeah, sure, it's true that often the difference between success and failure is in the attitude, the enthusiasm, which is another way of saying the amount of passion that you put into the thing," I agree.

"You've surely heard the stories about the skinny, ordinary woman who lifted a truck weighing several tonnes which was squashing her child? We know that under normal circumstances, she simply would not have the strength to lift that vehicle, but when it was absolutely necessary to save her child's life, she found the strength. Now, where does that strength come from?"

"We do not know with scientific certainty," I reply to Ralph, "but we usually say that it comes from what you are calling spirit, or passion or heart."

"Precisely. We don't know what to call it, but we all have sufficient experiences in our lives to know that it exists. Now, back to this productivity business. Think for a moment about all of the different productivity measures we use in companies. Now, think of the 3 parts to a human being we've just mentioned. Body, mind, spirit. What have we historically been measuring?"

"Interesting, your question. I suppose that we have been measuring the effective use of the time of the body. We do not consciously consider the other 2 parts. I don't think that it is because of any bad intent: it's just we haven't questioned ourselves enough to see if there is a better way to manage businesses. That's the way we've always done it, and I guess it will be the way we will carry on doing it until some brave companies show the way forward with another system, or until external market forces force us to make dramatic changes. And, judging by your argument of the rate of change statistics, we are already in this scenario."

"Andy, don't bother wasting your time trying to defend the why and wherefore of the current system, because I am not criticizing it, I'm just having a conversation with you about my beliefs. I want to tell you something. I met a gentleman called Sid Joynson in England. Sid has a dramatic way of expressing what we've been talking about. He says that in a typical company, it is as if there are invisible rays which criss-cross the entrance gate to the company. These rays have the job of extracting the hearts and minds of the workers while they are crossing over the gate entrance, and they deposit these organs in a special basket to one side. The workers go in and just contribute to the company the physical use of their arms and legs during the time they are there.

When they leave for home at the end of the day, those same mysterious rays replace the hearts and brains in the bodies of their rightful owners. As you quite rightly say, this phenomenon is not a conscious decision by the company, but it is however something like the result. Remember that even Jesus on the cross said: 'forgive them, Father, for they know not what they do'. So, we are not blaming companies for this unconscious behaviour; we are just extending an invitation for a change in the paradigm of management."

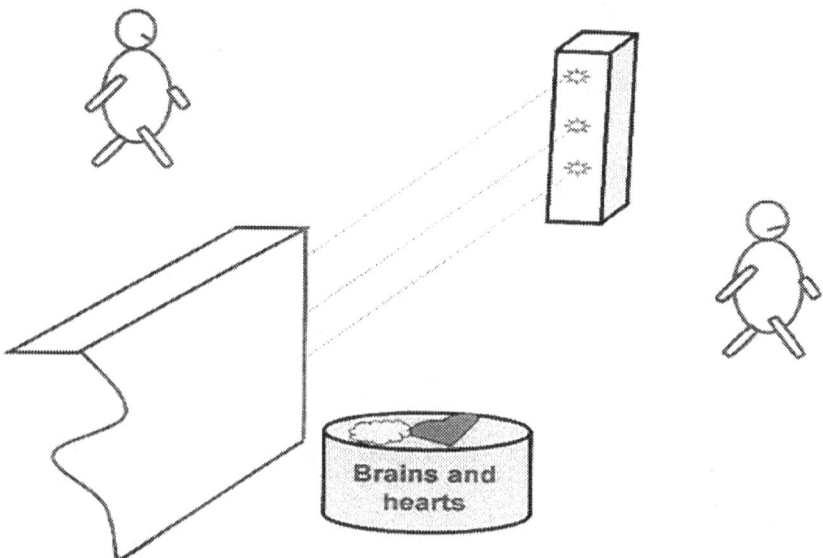

"Ralph, we've spent the whole morning talking about the theoretical side, so to speak, of the Champions' Workshop. And finally you have convinced me that there should be a great deal more that we can do with our people. What about a break from the topic for now and after lunch we can talk about putting it into practice?"

"Sounds like a great idea!"

With that, we go to lunch.

Chapter 9. The Champions' Workshop

After lunch, we resume our planning for the Champions' Workshop.

"Any other chains, while we're on the topic?"

"Yes", says Ralph. "These are often the very same company rules, systems and procedures, which once upon a time were probably set down as guidelines, but over time they become so entrenched that the workers do not even dare to question whether they make sense or not. Usually, the reasons why these rules were established in the first place no longer apply, and they stifle the workers' ability to produce excellence. And once we get their confidence going, you just watch those silly barriers fall down. This is usually one of the first areas to be tackled in a Workshop."

"So, out of the 3 days of the workshop, how long do you spend on de-brainwashing the workers out of their lifetime of their social conditioning?" I ask, now very intrigued about how this guy thinks he can achieve what seems impossible to me.

"I usually find that the first day is enough. If the workers are not at a point that they can accept that they are the real experts in their company, then it is unlikely that I would proceed with day 2 and day 3."

"Well, supposing that they do accept it, talk me through days 2 and 3, now," I ask Ralph.

"By this stage, we have broken some chains or fears and disempowering beliefs, and we have demonstrated that the 'biggest room in the world is the room for improvement'. Now is the time to start exercising creativity, and again a few exercises help to limber up the brain muscles. We form 4 to 5 teams of workers, and they set about choosing the areas they wish to work on. When their projects have been approved as meeting the 6 conditions specified earlier (faster; with less cost; better quality; safer; more fun; and no additional cost to the company), the teams are free to go back into the plant or their work areas to take their measurements of the current situation that they wish to improve. They return and tabulate their results. Then they work on their proposals, on the practical implementation details. This often requires a further visit to the field to take measurements of their proposed situation, sometimes achieving an instant implementation! They return with their results, and proceed to tabulate them as comparisons with the existing situation. Thereafter the teams of workers prepare their project presentations to the management teams."

"I should imagine that the presentation of their ideas to management is a very important part of the Workshop. Even if it is a brilliant idea, if it is not well presented, it can die a premature death," I comment.

"Entirely right," says Ralph. "An important part of the Workshop is teaching the workers how to get their point across to management in a way that grabs and retains the attention of the management team. On many occasions, workers know the problems and also know the solutions to those problems, but are not able to express themselves to managers so that the managers can readily understand them. Many times I've worked with groups of workers who told me that some of the ideas we were working on had already been suggested one time or another to management, but their ideas had not been accepted. I came to conclusion that managers reject ideas presented by workers not because they are bad, but often because of the way the worker presents the idea. Remember that the worker and the manager have been trained to think in different ways, and it is in the gulf between their thinking styles that many good ideas fall. For example, the worker may say to his manager: " hey boss, I've got a great idea which will make the work easier." The manager probably thinks: 'he's just looking for a way to make his life comfortable. I don't have time for this rubbish.' Now, if the worker were to change the way he presented his idea, for example: 'hey boss, I've got a great idea which would increase output in my line by 15 %, reduce rejects by five percent, and mean that the work is easier as well. Do you want to hear it?' The manager will undoubtedly say, 'yes, of course', because now the worker has spoken his language: a dramatic summary headline, a quantified result. So we do indeed spend quite a bit of time organizing the projects for presentation for success."

"And when is the presentation?"

"Usually at the end of day 3, or on the morning of day 4, depending on the availability of workers on shifts, and the management team."

"What type of workers do you want on the workshop?" I ask.

"It would be ideal to have between 20 and 25, taken from all areas. For example, you could include 2 from each of the 5 Production departments, 4 or 5 from maintenance, and the rest from the warehouses, despatch, quality control and administration. You can even include some people from sales if you want, even though your objective is to get projects which help towards the overall 30% productivity improvement target. Just try to avoid taking too many from any one area, unless you want to concentrate specifically on that area.."

"Can I include some supervisors?"

"Better not, we can schedule a separate session prior to the workshop for them, so that they understand and support the process. In my experience, as soon as you include someone from a higher level, the workers do not open themselves up, they feel all the while that someone from their bosses' ranks is watching and evaluating them. Also, the supervisors tend to try to take a dominant role, and that is precisely against the point; the workers have to come to accept that they, not the supervisors, are the experts."

"What else do you intend to cover with the supervisors?"

"Well, I often include some of the material to be found in the cassette tape program called 'The Psychology of Achievement' by Brian Tracy, a

Canadian motivational expert. Tracy points out that most managers and Supervisors believe that criticizing their people or a particular aspect of their behaviour will motivate them to improve. In fact, Tracy says, the opposite is true. People tend to avoid doing those things which lead to criticism, instead of trying to improve those things. He goes on to say that it would be better to take a sledgehammer to a piece of office furniture and destroy it, as it is more profitable for the company than to criticize a subordinate. You can easily and quickly buy a new office table. But when a manager criticizes, he wounds the self-esteem of the person criticized, and it takes many months of strenuous effort to recover that person's confidence, if at all. So rather than adding value to people, criticism has the effect of taking it away."

"Interesting. Another paradigm shift! Well, I'm clear about everything. I will schedule the workers for the 3 days and the presentation for next Monday at 9 a.m. So as we don't lose too much production, is it okay if we programme at least one of the 3 days over a weekend?"

"No problem. It's quite a normal request. Now that everything's set up, can you also fix me a session with the supervisors, so that they understand and support this process?"

"Sure thing. I'll get onto it."

XXXX OOOOO XXXX

At the beginning of the first day of the Workshop, I find myself with Ralph in our amply sized training room, where Bill Braces is finishing off his opening speech to a group of 25 workers selected by my supervisors.

"Many of you I have known for years, and even though we have some of the finest machinery in the industry, I consider that you people are the real assets of this company. Machines lose their value over time; you know that your car is worth less this year than it was worth last year.

But with people it is different. A worker's value should increase over the years, as long as he is acquiring more knowledge, wisdom and experience. And this Workshop is a way of helping you increase your value, to your company and to society. From what Ralph has told me about this course, I know that many things you will find useful in your personal lives, not just here at work. So, to finish off, my advice to you all is to really get involved in this, and I am keen to see what you produce by our next meeting on Monday morning. Good luck, and enjoy it!"

Bill and I then leave with a grin and a wave to Ralph, and the workshop begins. I had asked Ralph whether I could participate as an observer, but he was emphatic in refusing the presence of anybody associated with the hierarchy of the Company. He argued that he wanted the people to feel totally free to open up, and if that meant criticizing their superiors, then it should be allowed to happen. He believes that people will not be so free with their opinions if they feel that a 'management spy' is among them. The best way to circumvent this problem is to have someone neutral from outside the company, who is not seen as a management lackey. So I was not a witness to the actual process, but I was to the results.

Even when a manager means well (i.e. he criticizes because he genuinely thinks that this will help his subordinate to improve), he achieves precisely the opposite. We saw an example of just that, in this first Champions' Workshop at SportsBall, despite the prior session that Ralph had with the supervisors!

What happened was that at the start of the second day a lady worker, by the name of Marge, failed to turn up. It turned out that her supervisor, Jack, had brought her to tears at the end of the previous day, simply because he questioned her rather pointedly and aggressively about some figures she was collecting for the project her team was working on. She had left his office crying, and later sent a message that she didn't want to carry on in the Workshop because she was afraid of losing her job. When he was told why Marge had decided not to continue, Ralph left the teams to their work and went directly to Bill Braces' office. I should mention that, before starting the workshop, Ralph had agreed with Bill that Bill would make himself immediately available in the event of a 'people emergency', as he had put it. So, when Ralph asked Bill's secretary to interrupt his meeting, Bill came down to the shop floor to speak with Marge personally, to give her a personal assurance that her job was not at risk, and to ask her to continue on with the workshop. Bill readily accepted the task, and was sincere in his talk with Marge, with the result that she agreed to continue on with the Workshop.

The next day, when Bill and I questioned Jack about his part in the affair, he expressed surprise that Marge had been crying. All he had been trying to do, he said, was verify the figures she was collecting, and was totally unaware that she had left his office crying. For the first time perhaps, he became sensitive to the needs and feelings of his people, and started to adapt his supervisory style. He was somewhat successful in this: performance in his department improved, and he was in the subsequent months promoted to Shift Manager.

This was the only hiccup reported during the 3 days. The only other visible signs that something curious was going on was that groups of enthusiastic and motivated workers were going around the plant taking measurements and interviewing people.

At 8:45 a.m. on the fourth day, I arrive early and see that the workers are assembled in the training room, awaiting the arrival of the rest of the management team, and making final touches to their presentations. There is an air of good humor, tinged with nerves. The workers lay out their flipcharts in order of presentation. At 9 o'clock on the dot enter Bill Braces, Peter Greaves representing Human Resources, and three other members of the management team, Margaret Riley representing Quality,

George Barnes from Maintenance, Tom Burke from Planning, and Brian Rogers representing Sales. Ralph opens:

"Welcome to the performance improvement presentations by the Champions of SportsBall Inc.!"

The first team, which calls itself 'The Unbeatables' presents a project to reduce rejects on line 3 by 30%, by incorporating some simple practical procedures into the sequences carried out by the workers in the previous process. At the end of the 7 minutes of flipchart presentation, Margaret Riley asks how do they know that their procedures will work. Bob Dole, a stitching line worker, replies on behalf of the group: "First we interviewed the workers from that section, and they agreed with us to try out the changes. Then we did a trail run with them for over two hours. The normal material loss during an average two hours is 120 m2, and using our suggestions the workers, during the two hour trial, only recorded 60 m2 which is a 50% reduction, so we are saying 30% to be on the safe side."

Enthusiastic applause follows as the group concludes their presentation and return to their seats. The second team has called itself "The Better Halves", apparently because 3 of its 4 members are women. The lone male representative is a maintenance mechanic. This team proposes two projects. The first is a 27% production improvement on line 1, based on reducing the time lost due to line stoppages. What happens, the workers explain, is that each time the worker on the line has to walk from one part of the circular line to the other extreme, he has to stop the line, because he cannot leave his position running unattended. The workers calculate that the time lost due to these stoppages could be reduced by half, by shortening the distance that their colleague has to walk. This can be achieved by providing a door in middle of the line. The mechanic explains that a door can be placed there without disrupting product flow, and that there are several doors currently unused in the plant, and so there is no cost involved in the idea. The second project is to improve energy usage on the boiler by 16%, by having someone start work one hour earlier to make sure the boiler is turned on and at temperature when the lines start up. The only comment from the management team was from George Barnes, who said: "Good ideas, we'll get them installed over the coming weekend! No, better still, this afternoon!"

The third team introduces itself as "The Thinkers", and includes among its five members a salesman and a worker from the dispatch warehouse. They present a project to improve customer service through reducing the time taken from filling in the Sales Note until the products are dispatched, from 48 hours to 17, by eliminating 8 of the 17 steps involved in the process. Brian Rogers was suitably impressed, and to my great satisfaction, speechless.

The fourth team proposes a project to increase production on line 2 by 15%. The problem, they explain, is that the line stops for 10 to 15 minutes each hour, as it runs out of raw materials at the in-feed, and the operator usually has to go looking for the forklift driver to get him to bring another pallet. There is only enough space at the in-feed for one pallet, and the operator has to insert the components by hand. They suggest that a small conveyor be attached to the machine in-feed, with enough space for three pallets, so that the line won't stop and the forklift driver could calmly bring 3 pallets once each hour, instead of one every 20 minutes currently. Bill Braces says: "I can see why your project would work, but I understood that one of the conditions was that there was to be no cost involved." The electrician in the team replies: "remember last year when we sold the old LeatherMeister machine? I checked in the maintenance stores, and we kept the old conveyors to that machine, which if we gave them a 2-inch base, would do perfectly for the in-feed on line 2. So, there's no real cost involved." A hearty round of applause accompanies this group as they return to their chairs.

The last group goes by the name of "SportsBall Mad", and introduces a project to increase productivity, measured in balls per hour, in the cleaning & degreasing department by 100%, by bringing the degreaser to the production line and working there directly, instead of the current practice of batching up the balls to take them to the clean / degrease area twice a shift. The only question asked by a manager relates to the collection of the effluents, and this is explained by a novel but simple change to the suction cup on the degreasing machine, coupled with the revelation that there is a drainage pipe within meters of the work area, which has been covered up and left unused for at least the last 5 years.

At the end, I stand up to thank the workers for their enthusiasm and their contributions. "I have never been to a presentation before where the minimum improvement proposed in a specific area is 15%. Fantastic, guys! At a rough guess, I would estimate that these projects, when they are all implemented, as they will be, will give a 5 to 7% productivity improvement across the plant as a whole. Well done!"

Bill Braces sums up the meeting: "You have surpassed my expectations. I am impressed and pleasantly surprised by the variety of your projects, and by the solutions proposed. They are all simple, yet ingenious. You have confirmed that you are indeed the experts in the business, and have given me even more confidence in this company, its people and its future."

With smiles all around, these words from Bill close SportsBall's first Champions' Workshop.

"If you think education is expensive, try working out the cost of ignorance" - Brian Tracy

"If the rate of change outside your Company is faster than the rate of change inside your Company, then the end is in sight." - *Jack Welch, C.E.O. of General Electric*

Chapter 10: Be proactive, be facilitators

"So, congratulations on a very successful step two. The Champions' Workshop was a blast! And the news has spread like wildfire… I would say that there is a new level of enthusiasm in the plant, and the fear of job losses associated with change, such as the imminent introduction of the MultiStitch machine, appears to have been reduced dramatically, at least for now. So, now you want me to advance step three, the Product Flow and Activity Analysis, with the supervisors? Coffee with sugar?" I ask Ralph the next day, over a morning coffee in my office.

"Yes, if you would be so kind. This will sound a bit of a mouthful, so let's go through it step-by-step," explains Ralph.

"Well, you will have to train me very well so that I can lead the supervisors on this." I say. It was one thing for Ralph to do the Champions' Workshop on his own, but this one was mine!

"Don't worry, Andy, I have every faith in your abilities. And I believe that the best way for anyone to learn is to teach what they know to others. The procedure is not difficult, it just requires clear thinking and patience. And I'll talk you through it step by step. There are 8 steps to the procedure. I've laid them out on a sheet of paper for you. Here they are!"

Ralph hands me a single sheet, with the strange title, '*Training Program for Proactive Supervisors and Facilitators*'. Before reading it, I ask Ralph: "Why this long title?"

He replies: "One of the potential dangers involved in unleashing the workers' power through a process like the Workshops we've done, is that the supervisors feel threatened, and there is a risk that they will try to sabotage the process, consciously or unconsciously, believing that it is the best way to protect their interests. In fact, the supervisor's job is not under threat, only the NATURE of his job. A common paradigm of the 20th Century was that the supervisor is a cross between a policeman and an expert. He was there to ensure compliance to procedures, and the workers were merely economic units, like machines or tools, that he needed to get the job done.

The paradigm of the 21st Century is that the supervisor considers that his workers are the real experts, and his task is that of a facilitator or coach, whose main purpose is to create the optimum conditions so that his experts can deliver excellence and delight to the customer. It's a bit like being coach to, say, Pete Sampras. The coach is not the expert. In a game of tennis between the two of them, Sampras would probably beat his coach 6-0, 6-2 and 6-1, without too much sweat. Because he's the expert. But the coach can add value to his expert, and he does. He analyzes in an objective way all those factors which prevent his expert from reaching excellence, determines what are the training programs necessary to overcome or reduce these factors, and implements them. In short, he is constantly looking to provide the best conditions so that his expert can bring out the best of himself."

"Ok. That explains what you mean by the word 'facilitators'. But what does 'proactive' mean here?"

"Do you remember when we saw the short interval scheduling system, which is designed to identify problems as soon as they occur, in order to reduce or eliminate them , right? Well, going back to our tennis analogy, it is like our tennis coach giving Sampras advice *DURING* the game itself (instead of only when the game is over, when it's too late!), when he sees how his expert is responding to his opponent's strategy. If he identifies and eliminates a problem while it is happening, he is being proactive."

"So there are 2 sides to being proactive: firstly, it involves some element of planning to try to ensure that known problems will not happen, or if they do, the expert knows exactly how to deal with them; and secondly, during the action itself, whether it is a production run or a tennis game, being on hand to help overcome those problems which cannot be foreseen."

"A very good way of expressing it, Andy. You catch on fast."

"OK, Ralph. What a long explanation for a single line!" It's fun to pull Ralph's leg, when I feel he is getting too serious! "Well, let me read the rest of this document, now."

On the sheet, I read:

Procedure for reducing Muda to increase Value Added

1.   Map out the process (or a part of the process of special interest) followed by one of the key products on its physical journey through the company.

2.   Classify each step in the process mapped out according to the following:
• when work is being physically performed on the product,
• when the product is being physically transported,
• when the product is waiting to enter into a process,
• where the product is waiting at the end of the process before being transported to the next.

3.   For the journey mapped as described above, include the actual distances traveled, the amount of time spent, the number of people involved, the amount of product produced, the amount of materials used, and the inventory levels at each step in the process.

4.   Identify the bottlenecks within the process.

5.   Draw up an implementation plan to correct the excessive amounts of time, distances, material usage and inventories identified, particularly for the bottlenecks.

6.   Draw up an Activity List for the operators in the bottleneck areas.

7.   Apply the following five filters or questions to each activity in the activity list:
• Can the activity be eliminated?
• Can the activity be combined with other activities?
• Can the activity be modified to reduce its time?
• Can the activity be automated?
• Can the activity be delegated to employee of lower cost?

8.   Draw up an implementation plan of the changes necessary.

"Well, I've read through the list, but I'd like you to talk me through it now, please."

"Ok, Step 1. Mapping out the product flow. I suggest that you find yourself a nice large roll of brown paper, you know that type used for wrapping packets or boxes, and stick three meters length of it up on a wall where you'll have easy view of it. Take a representative product, for example, the football. We will start to draw out the process flow that the football takes through the factory, during its manufacture. We can start off with the reception of raw materials, and their storage in the raw material warehouse, or we can start off from the moment that the raw materials are issued from the warehouse to production, which is probably simpler at this stage. So, let's say that on day zero, hour zero, the raw materials warehouse receives a material requisition document from production. How long does it actually take from the moment that the requisition is written out to when the raw materials warehouse receives it? From the moment the warehouse receives the requisition, how long does it take until the raw materials are delivered to where they are needed in production? Of course, it is useful if you write down the quantities of the raw material involved. What distance do the raw materials travel between the warehouse and the first process in production? *How* are they transported? How long do they wait at that first process before being worked on? Once they enter the process, how long does it last? What scrap or rejects are produced during the process? At the end of the process, what quantities come out? And how long do they wait there, before being transported to the next step? For each stage of the process, we take the live document, showing the actual quantities of what happens, and stick this document onto the brown paper. Do you see what we're doing here? We are recreating in a visual form the life story of a football as it passes through all the stages of its production cycle. Here is a photograph of what a finished process map might look like:"

"You will notice that it is not meant to be a presentation document; the appearance really does not matter here. Pragmatism is more important than presentation. What is important is to get a visual representation of how information and product flow through the system, and quickly. Speed is of the essence, so do not even ask the supervisors to draw nice neat connecting lines with rulers; freehand lines are more than good enough. Then ask the supervisors to analyze the system for weaknesses, writing their comments, or critique points as I call them, onto the paper in their own handwriting, preferably in red ink so that it stands out. You've heard it said that people resist change; well, I think it's not true: people resist being changed. But when you involve people as active participants in the change process, they do not resist change, but embrace it. Once they have agreed on the system weaknesses, and they will stand out once you represent the system in this visual way, the corrective actions necessary almost become self-evident. And that's also where your help comes in."

"Ok," I say, "I think it's clear, and anyway if I have any queries later on I'll just call you. The rest of the steps are also quite clear to me, except for this one, number 6. What is an Activity List?"

"Nothing complicated", says Ralph, "You simply list each and every *activity* that a key person in a bottleneck area does. Once you've done that, then you can look at each activity carefully to see how many of the five filters you can apply to it, which is step 7. Let's make up an example. Let's imagine that you want to see where you can improve a salesman's performance. We'll use this sample sheet I have here."

Ralph pulls out a document from the wad in his briefcase, and quickly writes on it, before passing it to me. This is what he shows me:

ACTIVITY ANALYSIS

Position studied: **Salesman**

Ref	Activity Description	Unit of Measure	Frequency	Volume	Estimated time per UoM	Total estimated time
1	visit client	visit	Daily	5	60 mins	5 hours

He continues: "First of all, list in the column 'Activity Description', every activity in the form of a verb and a noun. For example, "insert (verb) mould (noun)", or "inspect (verb) component (noun)", or in this case 'visit client'. You then decide the '*Unit of Measure*' for each activity, for example 'pattern' or 'sheet' or 'meeting' or 'phone call' or in this case, 'visit' would be appropriate. Then you decide the *frequency* of the activity, i.e. in what time period does it occur. For example, the frequency of 'insert pattern' could be 'per shift' or 'daily', or 'weekly' or so on. In the case of our salesman, he makes sales visits every day, so the frequency is daily. Then you write down how much is the '*volume*' of work, i.e. how many times that activity occurs in the time period you specified, for example, 5 times per shift, 3 times per week, and so on. Our imaginary salesman makes 5 visits per day. Then you write down the *'estimated time'* it takes to do 1 of your Units of Measure, for example, 10 minutes for 1 pattern, 30 minutes for an inspection, etcetera. This salesman takes an average of 60 minutes for every client he visits. And finally, you bring it all together to see how heavy that activity weighs in terms of the total time requirement set on your key person in the bottleneck area. You simply do this by multiplying the volume by the estimated time. This allows you to rank the activities in terms of time required."

"So, in this example, the salesman spends an estimated 5 hours a day on sales visits, because he does 5 visits and each one takes 60 minutes." I like to make sure I'm crystal clear.

"Precisely. Obviously, you can carry the analysis on, and work out the same for his other activities, such as 'writing meeting reports',
'travel to client or back to office', or 'telephone client to set meeting', or 'process order' etcetera, and you would fill out his whole day. But let's carry on just with this activity, and see if we could apply any of the 5 filters. The first filter is: **Can the activity be eliminated?** Probably not in this case of a salesman, unless you are in a business where face-to-face contact between people is not that important. The second filter is: **Can the activity be combined with other activities?** You may wish for the salesman to assume some debt collection activities, or to check the client's inventory or to produce the order form during the meeting itself, instead of afterwards, sitting in his car. The third filter is: **Can the activity be modified to reduce its time?** You may believe or suspect that 60 minutes for a sales visit is too long, and upon investigating further, you discover that the salesman allows 60 minutes for each meeting, because on average his customers keep him waiting from 20 minutes to half an hour. You dig further, and you find that invariably the customers who keep him

152

waiting are usually those with whom he has not arranged the meeting by telephone prior to leaving his office. So one of the things you instigate is that the salesman confirms every meeting by telephone the day before. The fourth filter is: **Can the activity be automated?** The answer is probably no, but you could consider receiving orders over the internet. The fifth filter is: **Can the activity be delegated to an employee of lower cost?** Here, you investigate and find that the salesman spends the same amount of time with his 10 key customers, which represent 80% of his sales, as he does with the 40 others, which only represent 20% of his sales. So, in addition to helping him reprogram his time to dedicate more time to his key accounts, you could take the smallest accounts and assign them to a recently recruited junior salesman, for example.

So, you can see that this is a tool which allows you to focus your questions, as you seek to eliminate or reduce the effect of each activity. Do you have any questions?"

"No, I've gotcha" I say, "It's clear, and anyway if I have problems I'll call you. When are you planning to come back and follow up on our progress?".

"I'll be here again in about one month. Is that ok for you, or do you feel it is too soon?"

"No, that's great. See you next month, then."

"Best of luck.".

Chapter 11: The Follow-up

As it turned out, Ralph telephoned to request delaying his return visit by 2 weeks. I was not too upset because we had been as busy as I can remember. With all the work we've done, after implementing all the initiatives which came out of the Champions' Workshop and the supervisors' groups, and in the 6th week of running with the new system, we have some good news for him; we have just hit a 30% productivity increase, some 4 and a half months ahead of the schedule imposed on us by Bill! And all of this before buying and installing the new MultiStitch machine! As a matter of fact, I discovered that Bill is now reevaluating whether to proceed with the purchase.

We convene a large meeting, with most of the supervisors and several key workers to present our progress to Ralph, and we have also invited Bill. There are smiles all round. A long cry from 6 weeks ago, when my people were deflated and demotivated after Bill had criticized our 5% productivity increase. That was in week 28 (we operate a week number system, obviously there being 52 in the year).

We are now in week number 35. We have calculated Equivalent Unit factors for all of our products, and have calculated back 6 weeks prior to Ralph's arrival to see what our production was expressed in EUs, before running with our new systems. These 6 weeks we call the 'Base'. We related the EUs to the man-hours worked, and found an average ratio of 0.4 EUs / man-hour worked, which was not too far off my original Shaping and Stitching Dept calculation. During those 6 weeks of the 'Base', the productivity ratio had hovered around the 0.4 mark, but since then it has crept progressively upwards, until last week we hit 0.52, the 30% increase Bill requested (ordered!). The hours worked have dropped slightly, as there are less panic orders to be filled now, and overtime hours have dropped. Normally, there would be complaints from the workforce about this, but the new productivity bonus scheme more than makes up for it.

From week 28 onwards, we are now converting our production records to include the EU measurement as well as the traditional balls measure, and as we have incorporated more and more volume which was previously subcontracted, the EU indicator has been creeping up.

After welcoming Ralph back, Barry offers, as usual, to be a spokesperson. He presents the following graph:

3-part Productivity Graph

EQUIVALENT UNITS

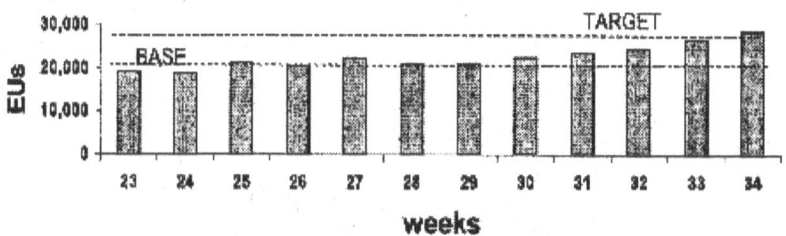

MAN HOURS WORKED: PRODUCTION

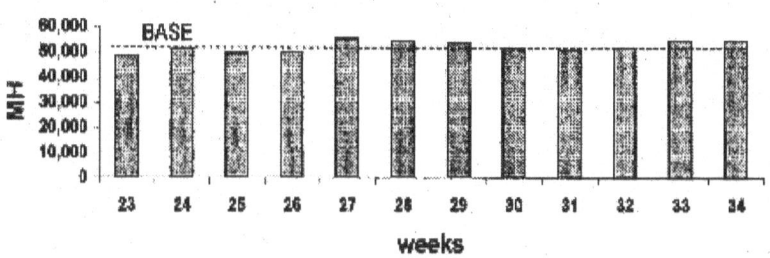

PRODUCTIVITY RATIO: EUs / Manhour

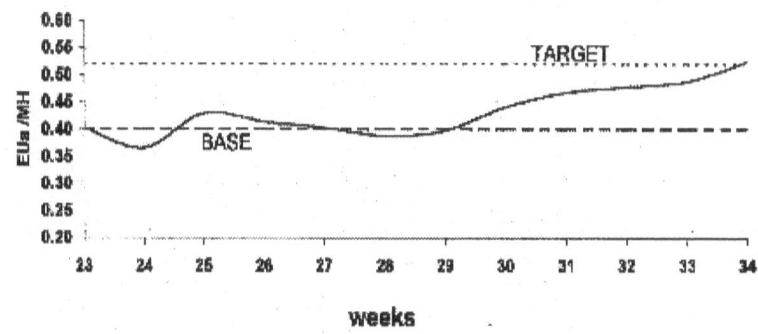

"A 30% improvement in 6 weeks! That's great, Barry! Well done, everyone. But what has happened with customer service?" asks Ralph.

I reply, saying: "Well, your next stop is to come with me to our Monthly Planning and Review Meeting. Remember what a disaster it was the last time you attended?"

Ralph nods, and I get the impression that he looks a bit worried.

But the meeting is a total transformation. Brian Rogers seems almost to have to force the words out of his mouth. "I have to acknowledge that Production complied with the Production plans in excess of 90%".

And I am thinking, 'why can't you just say, congratulations, Production achieved 98% compliance to the Plan?' But I refrain from saying anything, as I want Ralph to form his own impressions. In my view, I do not need now to defend Production; the figures speak for themselves.

Rogers continues: "Our customer service levels have risen from 60%, as I reported in our last meeting, to around 85%."

Again, I think but restrain from saying aloud: 'you really don't like other people looking good, do you? We got 89% customer service! What's up with you?'

Rogers carries on delivering his report: "This has helped us to increase sales by 10% over budget, because we are reporting less lost sales through cancelled orders and of course, because of our recent aggressive marketing campaign."

Bill takes over. "Thank you for your positive Sales report, Brian. I think that we can safely say that the sales increase was largely due to our efforts to improve our customer service from the production end."

'Thanks Bill!,' I'm thinking.

But Bill is not finished yet: "Well done to all in Production. Of course, we are now able to reduce our stock levels. To date, we've reduced stock by 12% and customer service has still risen, during the same period.

Furthermore, our quality indicators have improved from 3% to 1.8%. A commendable achievement, and congratulations again to all."

Bill then asks Ralph to comment on the productivity progress, and Ralph is warm and lavish in his praise.

When the meeting finishes, I invite Ralph to accompany me on a plant tour.

He comments: "Levels of Muda are visibly down, which is obviously a healthy sign. But I hope that you are not going to rest on your laurels?"

"No chance, Ralph. We're having too much fun!"

The author can be contacted at:

Trinity Consultores Limitada, Marchant Pereria 201, Piso 9, Providencia, Santiago, Chile.

Tel: (56) 2 204 9464   Fax: (56) 2 245 9651

E-Mail: fintan.bohan@trinity-chile.cl

About the Author

Fintan William Bohan was born in Dublin, Ireland and educated in England where he completed his BSc. degree at Brunel University, and subsequently a double degree in England and France (Master of Science in "Design of Production Machines and Systems", at Cranfield Institute of Technology, England, and "Innovation et Resistance de Materiaux" at Université de Technologie de Compiègne, Compiègne, France).

After some years working for the automobile components manufacturer LUCAS, in England and France, Fintan entered into productivity improvement consultancy with the American company, Alexander Proudfoot, with whom he worked on projects in England, France, Singapore and Scotland. This was during the 1980s, when Margaret Thatcher's government effectively broke the power of labor unions in the U.K., and large-scale layoffs for productivity became the norm.

Following his time with Proudfoot, Fintan worked for a decade for a competing British company in the same field, Knox D'Arcy, rising to Country Manager level in Mexico, South Africa and Chile. Becoming increasingly unsatisfied with the human cost of the process of seeking out people reductions as a route to improved productivity, Fintan decided to form his own consultancy, Trinity, which would specialize in improving productivity in client companies through "Unleashing People Power" instead of eliminating people.

During his 19 years as a productivity consultant, Fintan has worked with more than 100 organizations of all sizes and industries, covering manufacturing, banking, hospitals, services, sales, insurance and financial companies. His list of client companies includes conglomerates such as Allied British Foods, Murray & Roberts, Peugeot, Philips, Sappi, Scotiabank, to small companies employing only 30 people. Fintan's career has taken allowed him to work across the many cultures, from England, Scotland., France, Singapore, ex.-Yugoslavia, Mexico, South Africa, Botswana, Zimbabwe, to Chile, Argentina and Peru.

Fintan currently resides happily in Santiago, Chile with his wife and three children.